Called
to
Follow

To My Dear Friend Bill: Grace and Peace

Bill

The Sermons of
William J. Holmes Jr.

This book was made possible through a generous
contribution from members of the Salem Black River Presbyterian Church. I wish to thank Lynn Berry, Louise Bevan,
Martha Greenway, Cathleen O'Brien, and Bill and Brenda
Remmes who gave freely of their time and talents with editing
and layout. As always, my wife Judy remains a constant source
of encouragement.

ISBN: 978-1516814015

Photo credit: Jimmy Wood

Introduction

The late George Buttrick, pastor of Madison Avenue Presbyterian Church in New York, once described the power of preaching. He said that it is "the power of the Christ who joins us in prayer, in our study, in the crafting of the words, and in the moment of proclamation. The most important question of the sermon should be, 'Did you encounter the Christ this morning?'"

Buttrick's words describe the faithful preaching of our dear friend Bill Holmes. In the congregations Bill served, those who gathered every Lord's Day encountered Christ in Bill's preaching, his prayers and most of all in his presence as their pastor. They encountered Christ because Bill had visited and prayed with and for them in the week before. They encountered Christ because Bill took seriously the Reformed ethos which calls us to serve God with the life of the mind, and because he had spent time in his study in reflection upon the Word. They encountered Christ because Bill understood the power of language and the art of words. They encountered Christ because, at the moment of proclamation, when Bill stood in the pulpit to preach, they knew that his words would be authentic, true, and grounded in the Gospel.

This collection of sermons by Bill Holmes is not just an assortment of his manuscripts. It is, in essence, a confession of faith: the faith of the church, and the faith of a pastor committed to love and serve the Lord. It is also a wonderful reflection of the gratitude and love for Bill shared by so many. It has been a personal joy and privilege to follow Bill in ministry here in Manning and at the Salem Black River Church. But the greatest joy is the friendship that we share, and that I cherish. I know that many others who know and love Bill, and who have been touched by his ministry, will treasure this volume. And I know that all who read these sermons will encounter Christ, again and again.

George G. Wilkes
Manning, SC
2015

Table of Contents

The Advent of the Word:
The True Light that Enlightens

This year I celebrated my fourth Advent and Christmastide in Decatur. Last week I thought about the first Advent and Christmas I spent with you. It was not a particular easy time for me. Judy and the children, you may remember, did not move to Decatur until after Christmas in order that the children could finish the fall quarter in school. I lived in a two room apartment at Columbia Seminary for two months until I could move my family to Decatur. I learned something that year about loneliness that so many people experience. Each of you sought to make those early days for me as pleasant as possible. I think that I ate lunch and dinner in your homes almost every day. Yet, I detested to go home to that empty and lonely apartment every night where there were no loud radio and television playing and no children arguing about taking their evening bath! How I missed Judy and the children.

I did not handle those long nights alone very well. I paced the floor. I spent a fortune on long distance telephone calls. I cried. I read into the "wee" hours of the morning, and some nights I did not sleep at all. When one faces new challenges alone, self-doubts arise! Soon one begins to question himself: "Did I make the right decision? Am I ready for such a challenge? Do I have what it takes? Will they like and accept me? Can I do what they expect of me? Will determination and hard work make up for youth and inexperience? Will I have the strength to handle conflict, criticism, and "un-signed" letters of complaint?"

I remember, in particular, one cold, sleepless December morning. Tossing and turning, I prayed for sleep, yet hoping that the alarm clock would soon ring so that I could rush to "The Square Table," where I would hear the voices of people hurriedly eating breakfast.

Suddenly a strange sensation shook me out of my sleepless struggle. It was as if a voice called me to the window. I opened one slat of the venetian blinds and pushed my nose against the cold window pane. The rays of the security light danced across the frost on the ground. A few leaves lazily drifted from those majestic oak trees on Columbia's campus. Once they met the frozen ground, the wind would send them on a joy ride across the icy lawn. The city lay in a complete silence except for an occasional "Early Bird" flight heading out over Stone Mountain. The white and glistening windshields of the cars in the parking lot reminded me that I needed to jump back under the covers of the bed. I stood still, silently shivering, as the cold air slowly seeped through the cracks in the sill. Then suddenly my eyes turned toward the eastern horizon. Through the bare limbs on the trees, I could see the first rays of the rising sun. The gold, purple, and orange colors of dawn began to paint the black sky of night. As the Psalmist said, "Weeping may tarry for the night but joy comes in the morning."

I cannot remember a time that I was so happy to greet the early morning hour as I was on that new day. The faint light of dawn, which grew brighter with each passing moment, began to shine into my darkness of loneliness, reminding me that the lonely struggle would end shortly. Soon I would find myself sipping coffee and reading the morning newspaper in the local restaurant while listening to the voices of harried businessmen and women complain about the soaring interest rates and the national crisis brought about by the criminal capture of our hostages in Iran. Never did I think that the voices of strangers could serve as a means of grace! The light of dawn on that December morning gave me hope and courage to try it one more day. As John Morrison has written in one of the great Advent hymns.

> The race that long in darkness pined
> Have seen a glorious light;
> The people dwell in day who dwelt
> In death's surrounding night.

In the Prologue of John's Gospel, we find our text for today: "In Him was Life, and the Life was the Light of men. The Light shines in the darkness, and the darkness has not overcome it." As Hoskyns says in his commentary, "As the sun gives light to the whole world, the Word of God is the true light that gives light to all people." The Logos, the Eternal Christ, embraced the human flesh of a baby born in Bethlehem and lived as the True Light which enlightens the darkness of our human struggle.

Twice in John's Gospels, Jesus refers to Himself as the "Light of the World." In the eighth chapter we read these words: "I am the light of the world; he who follows me will not walk in darkness, but will have the light of life" (8:12). In the ninth chapter, we discover these words: "As long as I am in the world, I am the light of the world" (9:5).

Standing at that cold window pane on that lonely December morning three years ago taught me several things about Jesus as the light which illumines the darkness of life.

First of all, the light which the Christ Child brought at His birth in Bethlehem is the Light which puts chaos to flight. In the Genesis account of creation, we read: "The earth was without form and void, and darkness was upon the face of the deep; and the Spirit of God was moving across the face of the waters. And God said, 'Let there be light; and there was light.'" As Professor Barclay says, "The new created light of God routed the empty chaos into which it came."

Since John's Gospel is the record of the new creation which offers men and women new life as the sons and daughters of God, Jesus, the Eternal Christ, is the light which shines into the darkness, the light which transforms the struggle of human existence into life. Jesus is the only person who can prevent life from becoming chaotic. Jesus is the only person who can change the chaos of life into meaning!

What is the chaos in your life? For me, on that cold December day, chaos was loneliness and separation. Perhaps the chaos which threatens to rule and ruin your life is illness or privation or indifference or unhealthy passion or uncertainty or worry or loneliness or rejection or hatred or fear or the new or the old or separation or disability. What is your chaos into which the Light needs to shine?

Christmas captures chaos with creativity! Jesus is born! The Light which enlightens the darkness of our lives is none other than the Logos, the Word, the Eternal Christ which moved across the face of the deep in the beginning, transforming "nothingness" into life and meaning. Christmas means that Jesus has come into your life and mine, taking the chaos of our lives upon Himself. He gives His life to our emptiness, His purpose to our meaninglessness, His Light to our darkness, His power to our weakness, His hope to our despair, His courage to our cowardliness. Christmas is standing at a cold window on a winter morning and realizing that you are not alone. Christmas is peering into the cold darkness, realizing that you can make it one more day. Christmas is joyfully receiving His Light into our darkness. Christmas is offering our chaos to Christ's creativity. As Charles Wesley so beautifully writes,

> Come Thou long-expected Jesus,
>
> Born to set Thy people free,
>
> From our fears and sins release us;
>
> Let us find our rest in Thee.

On Christmas, the Light of Jesus Christ shines into our chaos.

His Light brings newness and hope!

The second thing that I learned while standing and shivering at the cold window three years ago is that as the light of dawn becomes brighter, one can see the reflection of his/her face in the window pane. The light of day helped me to see some startling scenes. I saw myself as Judy would see me if she had been there: furled hair, unshaven face, swollen eyes from lack of sleep, and a despairing stare.

As Professor Kittel says, "The Revelation brings light to what a person really is. This is the crisis." The Light which the Eternal Christ brings in His birth at Bethlehem is revealing light. As the light of the rising sun revealed to me my unattractive face in the window pane, so the Light that Jesus brings to the world at Christmas is the Light which reveals the unattractiveness of our lives: our sin, our faithlessness, our hopelessness, our helplessness, our worry, our insecurity, our fear, our self-justification. We never see our faces as others see them until we look into a mirror or into a cold window pane. We never see our lives as they are until we see them in the light of Jesus.

His revealing Light illumines our need for God's grace. His revealing Light convinces us that we have no hope save in Him. His revealing Light leads us to God's forgiveness, love, acceptance, purpose, and strength. His revealing Light shines into the darkness of our sin and separation, and like the prodigal son, leading us to the welcoming arms of the Father.

Once again Charles Wesley enhances the celebration of Christmas with the words of one of his carols.

Hail, the heaven-born prince of Peace.
Hail the Sun of Righteousness.

Light and life to all He brings, Risen with healing in
His wings.

Mild He lays His glory by, Born that men no more may die,

Born to raise the sons of earth, Born to give them second
birth.

On Christmas, the Light of Jesus Christ shines on our faces and our lives, revealing our weakness and sin. His Light leads us to grace, to forgiveness, to acceptance, to newness of life.

The final thing that I learned on that cold day in December three years ago is that the light of a new day leads us away from window gazing, to the shower, to the breakfast table, to the office, to purpose. As I pushed open that heavy bronze door that leads one out of the protective confines of Florida Hall into the cold dark world, the fresh cold air invigorated my lungs and the warmth of the morning sun felt good on my cold face. Suddenly I realized that I was not alone. Suddenly I realized that I had made the right decision. Suddenly I knew that I could do the job. Suddenly I knew that I would find acceptance. Suddenly I felt that I could endure criticism. Suddenly I felt a guiding hand. Suddenly I knew what had to be done!

The Light which the Eternal Christ brings to the dark world at Bethlehem is a guiding light. John shares these words of our Lord: "Walk while you have the light, lest the darkness overtake you. He who walks in darkness does not know where he goes."

With the coming of Christmas, we receive the Light of Jesus which shines into the uncertainty and darkness of the future. We no longer have to guess. We no longer have to grope. We no longer have to walk on a dark path. The way becomes clear. The decisions that are often clothed in the doubt of night are illumined with the brightness and certainty of the "Sun of Righteousness."

The Light of Jesus and the Light of Christmas are a guiding Light. With the coming of Christmas, we find courage to enter into a new year. We can face new challenges, new problems, and new decisions with confidence, knowing that Jesus is the Light which guides our every step. When we receive His Light, we never have to walk in darkness. When we receive His Light, we can face an uncertain future. When we receive His Light, we never have to fear the facing of decisions. When we receive His Light, we have the assurance that Jesus goes before us like the pillar of fire which led the "chosen" through the wilderness wanderings. He will not forsake us! He will not disappoint us! He will lead us to the realization of what His Father has destined us to be! Those of us who must face uncertainty and decisions can do so with the confidence of Christmas Light, because He will not let us walk on a dark path.

As we sang a few minutes ago,

> Flocks were sleeping; Shepherds keeping
> Vigil till the morning new. Saw the glory,
> Heard the story, Tidings of a gospel true.

Thus rejoicing, Free from sorrow, Praises voicing

Greet the morrow: Christ the Babe was born for you.

Prayer

Eternal God, we are people who have walked in darkness of human struggle, and have seen a great light—Your Light. During this Advent and Christmas, let the Light of Your Word shine into our chaos, into our sin, and into our uncertainty, for we make this request, trusting in the Light, even Jesus Christ, our Lord. Amen.

The Advent of the Word:
John 1:14-18

Seeing some of the sights of human suffering in a nursing home often sends us away in angry tears. I never leave one of those places without questioning the providence of God: Why do some people have to experience and endure such an agonizing struggle?

Several months ago, I met an elderly man in the halls of one of the nursing homes. Seated in a wheelchair, he was a pathetic sight for eyes to behold. His fingers and toes were hideously swollen and crooked, ostensibly from arthritis. His tiny legs showed signs of atrophy from lack of mobility. With a curved back, he leaned forward with his face buried in his chest. One almost had to stoop to catch a glimpse of his face. As I walked by, I caught a glimpse of his blank stare. Saliva drooled down his chin, and his lips slowly moved in silent utterances. When I reached the end of the hall, I heard a painful shout. Turning to lift his weak arms heavenward, he helplessly cried, "O Jesus, where are You?"

His painful plea reminded me of Isaiah's inquiry: "Why don't you rend the heavens and come down?" When the mystery of God's presence and the mystery of life's suffering ways baffle us, we often find ourselves crying out, "O Jesus, where are You? Why don't you rend the heavens and come down?"

Edmund Sears in his Christmas carol, "It Came Upon the Midnight Clear," writes

> And ye beneath life's crushing load,
>
> Whose forms are bending low,
>
> Who toil along the climbing way with painful steps and slow,
>
> Look now! For glad and golden hours,
>
> Come swiftly on the wing:
>
> O rest beside the weary road,
>
> And hear the angels sing.

Those of us who bend under life's crushing loads can thank God for Christmas with its assurance that He has heard our cries of "Jesus, where are You?" In the Prologue, John tells us that God has responded to our pleas: "The Word became flesh and dwelt among us."

To understand John's concept of Christmas, one has to appreciate the historical context in which he wrote. John wrote to the early church in the Greek world which struggled to combat a heresy called Docetism. This heresy strongly asserted the divinity of Jesus, but members of that sect vehemently denied the humanity of our Lord.

The Docetists taught that Jesus only appeared to have human flesh. They believed that all human flesh was corrupt, and therefore, the Divine One would never taint himself with corrupt earthly flesh. Thus, Jesus, according to the Docetists, looked like a man, acted like a man, but he was never subject to all the limitations of earthly flesh, especially the limitation of death. After all, the Eternal One can never die, they believed. So the Docetists taught that Jesus did not come to this world to help us in our earthly struggle; rather they believed He came to help us escape from the prison of this world.

Responding to this heresy which denied the humanity of our Lord, John wrote, "And the Word became flesh and dwelt among us." When John wrote that the Eternal Christ became flesh, he did not mean that Jesus shared our sinful existence. Rather John meant that Jesus was a whole person, with both body and spirit; He embraced the flesh of human existence which God created in the beginning of time—the flesh which knew no sin.

The apostle Paul spoke against the Docetic heresy when he wrote, "In the fullness of time, God sent forth His son, born of a woman." In this respect, Jesus was just like any other human being: the Eternal Christ was born as you and I were.

When you and I affirm our faith with the Apostles' Creed, we confess, "I believe in Jesus Christ, His only Son our Lord; who was conceived by the Holy Ghost, born of the Virgin Mary." The statement "born of the Virgin Mary" not only emphasizes the deity of Jesus but it is an everlasting statement against Docetism. We believe that Jesus came into the world in the same manner as every person born of human flesh, with human flesh.

The Eternal Christ who became flesh was a real human being in all facets of life. He experienced hunger, thirst, fatigue, fear, suffering, and even death.

Luke tells us that our Lord's earthly knowledge was subject to our human limitations, "And Jesus increased in wisdom and stature, and in favor with God and man."

Our Lord experienced the human need to pray as any man or woman. When he faced death, Matthew tells us that Jesus wrestled with inner fear. Like any of us, he did not want to suffer and to die. In Gethsemane he prayed, "My Father, if it be possible, let this cup pass from me."

On the cross, Jesus experienced human separation from God— the separation of our sin. He prayed, "My God, why have you forsaken me?" In other words, "Where are you? Why don't you rend the heavens and come down?" One can find no stronger evidence for our Lord's humanity than in this painful plea.

Physically, spiritually, intellectually, and emotionally Jesus shared your humanity and mine. He laughed. He cried. He learned. He felt fear. He experienced loneliness. He died. He was one of us—a human being with flesh and feelings.

The author of Hebrews tells us that Jesus was a man who faced temptations: "He is one who in every respect has been tempted as we are." Our everyday Jesus faced temptations, the ones which we would prefer to hide this morning. If he had not experienced all of the doubts, pressures, and desires which lead us away from God, how could the writer of Hebrews say that Jesus "was able to sympathize with our weaknesses"?

Yet Jesus, the Eternal Christ, who "became flesh," never sinned. Such a statement prompts the following question: How can we call Jesus a human being if he did not sin? Is not sin part of humanity? No!

When God created the first Adam, sin was not a part of humanity. Sin entered human existence when the first Adam disobeyed God. So the second Adam came, i.e., Jesus, and he not only shared our human flesh and struggle in every facet of life, but he taught us the meaning of true humanity, a life in perfect obedience to God.

John does not stop with the statement, "And the Word became flesh." He goes on to say, "And dwelt among us." The clause, "dwelt among us" implies more than the English verb suggests. The Greek word for "dwelt" is derived from the Greek noun for "tent." When John wrote these words, he may have been thinking of the tabernacle in the wilderness where the Lord dwelt among His people. The Hebrew tent or tabernacle was the center of the manifestation of God's glory while the Exodus people wandered in the wilderness. As God visited His people in the tabernacle or tent in the wilderness, so he lived with us in the tent of human flesh.

A tent is usually a transitory dwelling. Thus John tells us that the glory of God, the presence of God, was with us for a short period of time in a human tent, in the earthly flesh of Jesus.

Christmas means that God sought a new dwelling with His people—a dwelling of human flesh. In Christmas, we experience the love and humility of God: "For God so loved the world," that He became a creature. He refused to be a prisoner of the spiritual realm, and He chose to live as one of us.

Christmas also means that God has placed His blessings on this earthly existence of human flesh. The name that He gave to the new tabernacle is "Jesus," which means "God helps." Christmas means that God not only offers salvation for our spirits, but He also desires a new creation for our bodies. God does not merely want us to look forward to the new heaven and earth, but He wants us to appreciate and to enjoy this earthly life of flesh through realizing the true humanity which Jesus lived—the life which God intended us to have in the beginning. God does not want us to escape this human life as the Docetists taught. He wants us to be human like Jesus. The early church father, Irenaus, once wrote, "He was made what we are that He might make us what He is Himself."

The name "Jesus" means "God helps." Christmas means that God has come in the tabernacle of Jesus' flesh to save us from the need to flee this earthly life as the Docetists taught. Christmas means that the Creator became a creature, not for the purpose of delivering us from the struggles of human flesh, but rather to give us the strength to face and to courageously endure the trials and struggles of human flesh.

How does Jesus help us to face and to courageously endure this struggle of human existence? This is John's answer: "And the Word became flesh and dwelt among us . . . and from Him we have received grace upon grace."

The literal translation of John's statement is this: "From Him we have received grace instead of grace." What does John mean by such a strange statement?

To understand John's words, one must appreciate the meaning of the word "grace." As one theologian has said, "The grace of God is an active and effective power from God bringing merciful aid to men and women. It signifies the energetic initiative which God has taken and still takes in Christ to heal the breach between humans and God, and to repair the ruin in our souls."

Grace is the power which Christ gives to us when we experience human pain and struggles so that we can courageously face and endure the problems. Grace is Christ's power to help us.

When the Apostle Paul cried out for God to either ease the thorn in the flesh or to remove him from this earthly tent, God responded, "My grace is sufficient. My power is made perfect in your weakness." We do not have to flee this earthly life, as the Docetists taught, because God is with us in His grace. God is with us in His power to help us to courageously face any problem with faith and strength. We are never alone. God is with us in all of our struggles with His grace, with His divine strength for us.

What does John mean when he says, "From Him we have received grace instead of grace." As Barclay says, "Grace is never a static reality. It is always a dynamic power which never fails to meet the situation. One need invades life and one grace comes with it. That need passes and another assaults us and with it another grace comes."

"Grace instead of grace" means that different situations in life demand a different type of grace. We need one grace in moments of prosperity and another grace in moments of adversity. We need one grace in moments of contentment and another grace in moments of discouragement and desperation. We need one grace to shoulder our own problems and another grace to bear the burdens of others. God is always present with us with grace to meet and to endure every problem in life. From him we have received grace sufficient to meet every need.

Christmas means that earthly life is good. Jesus has come to show us how to live that life to the fullest. Christmas means that this good life can present us with problems, and when they come, we do not have to withdraw or desire to flee for God is present with His gracious power which is sufficient for every need!

The next time we meet a person seated in a wheelchair who cries out, "Jesus, where are You?" or the next time we face an insurmountable problem and find ourselves crying out, "Why don't you rend the heavens and come down?" let us remind ourselves of John's concept of Christmas. Jesus has dwelt with us in the tabernacle of human flesh.

He knows what it is like to live a human life like ours. He knows what it is to face problems, pain, and suffering. Since He knows, He comes to us with grace instead of grace—strength and power sufficient to meet our every need. Since He comes with Christmas courage, we can say to each other, even in our painful situations, "Merry Christmas."

William Barclay, *The Gospel of John*, page 72.

Note: I am indebted to Shirley Guthrie for his interpretation of the humanity of Jesus. One may find a fuller explanation in his book, *Christian Doctrine*. Pp 226-241.

Prayer

Come Lord Jesus, come quickly and strengthen us for
the living of these days. Amen

Advent 1997
Veni, Vidi, Vici

I have always maintained a love for the classics, and from the classical era of history, a reader discovers the life of Julius Caesar, perhaps the greatest of all orators, politicians and military geniuses, ruling Rome from 49-44 B.C. However, on the Ides of March, 44 B.C., Marcus Junius Brutus and Gaius Cassius led a group of aristocrats in a plot to assassinate Caesar, fearing that he had gained too much power. From this story of historians, one remembers the dying words of Julius Caesar as he looked into the eyes of his friend, Marcus Junius Brutus and spoke in a gasping voice, *Et tu Brute?*

Julius Caesar was a monarch without a crown. Even though he was offered the crown on several occasions, he refused it, because the Romans despised kings. In one of his last military victories that made

Rome the center of an empire that stretched across all of Europe – the victory over Pharnaces II, King of Pontus – Julius Caesar in the spring of 47 B.C. sent a brief but meaningful message to the Roman Senate. These were his words: *Veni, Vidi, Vici.* I came, I saw, I conquered. These same three Latin words describe the life of our Messiah, the life of our Savior, and the life of our King, Jesus of Nazareth. I came, I saw, I conquered.

As far as we know, Jesus never spoke this particular sentence that comes from the lips of the triumphant Roman leader, yet his earthly life and ministry fulfill those words in such a way that no other earthly monarch can. "*Veni, Vidi, Vici.*" I came, I saw, I conquered. Who, but the promised Messiah, Jesus, the Son of God, could speak and live those words? I came, I saw, I conquered.

On the first Sunday in Advent I want us to consider the first word *Veni.* I came. The English word "Advent" comes from the two Latin words *Ad* and *Venio*, meaning "to come". For years Israel lived in feverish expectation, waiting patiently yet hopefully for the Messiah to come. In his great Advent hymn, Charles Wesley captures this period of waiting in these words:

> Come Thou long expected Jesus, Born to set Thy people free, From our fears and sins release us, let us find our rest in Thee. Israel's Strength and Consolation; Hope of all the earth thou art; Dear Desire of every nation, Joy of every longing heart.

Come thou long expected Jesus. And to that prayer, Jesus speaks:

"I came born a babe in Bethlehem's barn."

So let us turn our thoughts to the Latin word, *Veni* and the season of Advent. We discover Jesus speaking these words: "You say that I am a king. For this I was born, and for this I came into the world to testify to the Truth. Everyone who belongs to the Truth listens to my voice."

Obviously we recognize these words of Jesus as a portion of a dialogue betwixt Pilate and our Lord. The setting is the procurator's praetorian, and Jesus is standing trial before the prefect. Lest one thinks that I have lost my sense of timing by proffering the Lenten text for the first Sunday in Advent, let me refer us to our Lord's words once again, words which He spoke only hours before His death: "You say that I am a king. For this I was born, and for this I came into the world to testify to the Truth."

So Jesus speaks Latin, as it were, to a Roman Procurator who studied the military history from Julius Caesar's campaigns and who was aware of Julius Caesar's words spoken after the victorious triumph in Pontus. *Veni*. I came. "For this I was born and for this I came into the world to testify to the Truth."

How well we remember the context of these words. Jesus, having celebrated the Passover in the Upper Room, departs from that glorious memorial meal to the shadows of Gethsemane where He prays in sorrowful agony. His prayers and the sleep of His less than watchful disciples are interrupted by a mob of Temple priests, carrying lanterns and swords. Arrested and bound, Jesus is taken to illegal kangaroo courts: first, to Annanias, and then, to Caiaphus. John fails to tell us what the synoptics reveal. In the trial before Caiaphus and the Sanhedrin, Jesus is accused and found guilty of blasphemy. Such a charge was an internal religious affair punishable by stoning. However, the high priest and members of the Sanhedrin maintained that capital offenses came under the jurisdiction of the Roman courts, so they took Him to Pilate, changing that charge from blasphemy to sedition, knowing full well that Pilate and Roman law yielded to religious courts in conquered lands.

Immediately Pilate attempted to extricate himself from the apparent parochialism of this case. "Take him and judge him according to your law."

However, the Jewish leaders maintained Jesus' guilt of sedition and Pilate, thus, was required to investigate such a charge. Having been accused of claiming himself as the Christ, King of the Jews, Jesus stands before Pilate in an eerie and calm silence. The Procurator then speaks to this battered and bound prisoner who claimed, according to his accusers, to be a rival of Caesar: "Are you the King of the Jews?"

Pilate's question is filled with incredulity. He cannot bring himself to believe that this man, humbly clad as he is, arrested and alone without an army to defend him can be making any pretensions to earthly and royal power. To Pilate's question, "Are you the King of the Jews?" Jesus answered, "Do you ask this of yourself or did others tell you this concerning me?" In other words, "Do you have a personal interest in asking about my kingship or do you ask only as a judge?"

Instead of the judge examining the accused, the accused examines the judge.

Angered by what Pilate infers as impertinence, he retorts angrily, "Am I a Jew? Your own nation delivered you up to me. What have you done?" There is no hesitancy in Jesus' answer, "My kingdom is not of this world; if my kingdom were of this world, my servants would fight to keep me from being handed over to the Jews. But my kingdom is not from here."

Without considering the import of our Lord's words, namely the issue of who or what Jesus really is, Pilate responds incredulously, "So you are a king?" It is at this juncture that we discover the text and lesson for this first Sunday in Advent.

Jesus speaks, "For this reason I was born, and for this reason I came into the world to testify to the Truth."

Pilate, acting like a confused schoolboy inquires, "What is truth?" At this point the dialogue ceases. Jesus proffers no answer to the procurator's inquiry: "What is truth?"

Bound, bruised and bleeding, our Lord stands before Pilate in majestic silence. Pilate discovers the answer to his question, for the one who is the Way, the Truth and the Life stares into the confused eyes of one Pontus Pilate, procurator of Judea.

In this text the Greek word "Truth" is *a-le-thia*, and for the Gospel writer John *a-le-thia*, Truth, is divine reality. What is Truth?

"For years", says Frederick Buechner, "politicians, scientists, theologians, philosophers and poets have attempted to tell Pilate, but the sound that they have made is like the sound of an empty bucket falling down basement steps. What is truth?"

Jesus does not answer Pilate's question. He just stands there. His silence is deafening. Somehow in this encounter, we see that neither Pilate nor any of us can understand truth. We need to experience it through Jesus, the truth, the divine reality. What is divine reality? Divine reality is God in the flesh of Jesus.

"For this reason I was born," said our Lord, "and for this I came into the world to testify to the truth."

Veni, "I came" to testify to the truth, to show you divine reality, to reveal the love, goodness, mercy and will of God. What does the word Veni mean to you and me this morning as we attempt to make ourselves believe that it is Advent once again and that Christmas is only three weeks from next Thursday?

Veni, "I came." Pilate is too blind to see what by grace we have been given to see—divine reality, truth, God in the flesh. *Veni.* "I came" implies or rather emphasizes the truth of Christ's pre-existence. I came into this world from another world, from heaven, from the holy presence of the Father.

John begins his Gospel with those immortal words of the Prologue: "In the beginning was the Word and the Word was with God and the Word was God. The same was in the beginning with God. All things were made by Him; and without Him was not anything made that was made."

Or as the apostle wrote to the Colossians: "Jesus is the image of the invisible God, the firstborn of every creature. For by Him were all things created and He is before all things."

In essence, Jesus is saying to Pilate, "Before you were a thought in God's mind, I lived. Before Abraham was, I am." Jesus is God, the son of God, who has dwelt in the Godhead eternally. Julius Caesar cannot make that claim. Pontius Pilate cannot make that claim. You and I cannot make that claim. Only God is immortal. Veni, "I came" from heaven to show you the truth, divine reality; to reveal to you the salvation of God which existed even before the foundation of the world.

The word *Veni* has an additional meaning for us who suddenly find Advent descending upon us with an inexorable rush. The statement by Jesus, "For this I was born, for this I came," reminds us of the reason for the season; the incarnation. Although Jesus is eternal, existing before all things forever, He became human flesh, born of the Virgin Mary.

Hear the words of the Apostle which he wrote to the Philippians: "Let this mind be in you which was also in Christ Jesus: Who being in the form of God thought it not robbery to be equal to God, but humbled himself, taking upon himself the form of a servant, and was made in the likeness of men."

Or, as Charles Wesley writes in the familiar Christmas Carol:

> Christ by highest heaven adored; Christ,
> the everlasting Lord!
>
> Late in time behold Him come,
> To the earth from heaven's home;

Veiled in flesh the Godhead see; Hail the incarnate Deity,

Pleased as man with men to dwell; Jesus our Emmanuel.

Veni. "I came" from heaven, humbling myself by having human flesh. I came as Emmanuel, God with us in human form so that Godhead would always know what it is like to live in this difficult life of the flesh. Thus, you would know by what your eyes could see and your ears could hear who God is and what God is through the flesh of the only begotten Son.

The word *Veni* reveals to us the two natures of Christ, Jesus the Messiah is fully God and fully human. And He came to show us what we were destined to be in His perfect humanity. We humans learn what it means to be human as we imitate Jesus' life of human flesh. Finally, the words of Jesus, "I came", follow the words, "For this reason I was born." *Veni* "I came" means that Christ was born, and it is His birth for which we prepare during Advent, and it is His birth which we celebrate during Christmastide. The word *Veni* implores us to open our hearts to the birth of Him who is our Savior and to sing a song to Bethlehem.

As Luke writes:

> And lo, it was, that while they were still there the days were accomplished that she should be delivered. And she brought forth her first born son and wrapped him in swaddling clothes and laid him in a manger because there was no room for them at the inn. And there were in the same country shepherds abiding in the field, keeping watch over

their flock by night. And lo, the angel of the Lord came upon them, and the Glory of the Lord shown round about them and they were sore afraid. And the angel of the Lord said, 'Fear not for I bring you good tidings of great joy which shall be to all people. For unto you is born this day in the city of David a Savior which is Christ the Lord.

A savior which is Christ the Lord. And so Jesus speaks to you and me this morning: For this reason I was born and for this reason I came. *Veni.* I came to be your savior and to save you from your sins.

In the rush and busyness of these holy days of preparation, let us not forget the meaning of Christmas. Let us cling to that word. *Veni.* I came, I was born to be your savior: "I came that you may have life, and have it abundantly."

In the words of Bishop Brooks, "O holy child of Bethlehem, descend to us we pray. Cast out our sin and enter in. Be born in us today."

Veni. Vidi. Vici. I came. I saw. I conquered. Words which Julius Caesar spoke after the victory at Pontus in 47 B.C. Three years later, he lay dead at the hands of assassins. Only Jesus can speak these words, for He alone is God, not Caesar. And so He says to us throughout Advent *Veni. Vidi. Vici.* I came. I saw. I conquered. But His word to you and me on this first Sunday of Advent is *Veni.* I came for you and for you and for you.

The Lamb That Walked Away

Luke 2:1-20

As the final ray of evening's light disappeared under the blanket of night's darkness, Jeshua and Amar lay on the cold, damp ground of Bethlehem's plains, near the crackling of the campfire, gazing upward into the vast vault above them where twinkling stars often speak to the hearts of the restless.

Amar lay close to Jeshua, his cold nose pressed gently against Jeshua's neck and his innocent, wooly face rested lightly on Jeshua's shoulder. His soft, warm breath provided moderate heat for Jeshua's cold face, and his delicate fleece provided a protective covering for the boy's small, bony frame against the chill of a December night. Jeshua put his left arm around Amar's back as the two drifted off to sleep under heaven's watchful eye.

Jeshua and Amar were inseparable friends, and they had been for several months, since Amar's mother was killed by a prowling predator as she attempted to protect her young from the hideous death which she endured for Amar's sake. If you have yet to figure it out, Jeshua is a boyish shepherd, and the adopted parent, as it were, of Amar, the motherless lamb. Amar, I suppose, was appropriately named. In Hebrew, the lamb's name means "woolly."

However, on this particular night, sleep did not come easily to Amar's big, brown eyes or to the drooping, copper eyes of his shepherd friend. The busy movement on the horizon was too distracting. "In those days there went out a decree from Caesar Augustus that all the world should be taxed. And all went to be taxed, everyone into his own city." Those who were of the house and lineage of David made their journey to Bethlehem—the city of Israel's great king—to be enrolled as Caesar's taxpayers.

Sounds travel swiftly and strikingly through the still silent air when half-spent was the night. Cries of tired, hungry children echoed off the ancient walls of Bethlehem. The harness bells of camels rang merrily and methodically from the busy streets of David's city, and even the sounds of donkey hooves could be heard from the cobbled streets as endless processions of these humble beasts plodded patiently along one avenue after another.

All the sheep became restless from this unusual movement and these invading sounds. Jeshua's oldest brother began to play his flute in an attempt to calm the nervous flock, while Jeshua whispered some of the words of the shepherd's psalm into the flapping ear of Amar:

"The Lord is my shepherd, I shall not want. He maketh me to lie down in green pastures. He leadeth me beside still waters, He restoreth my soul. . .Yea though I walk through the valley of the shadow of death, I will fear no evil; for thou art with me; thy rod and thy staff they comfort me."

These ancient words seemed to soothe the anxious spirit of Amar and soon his small eyelids closed with heaviness, as did Jeshua's. However, their brief sleep was interrupted by a brilliant light which penetrated their sagging eyelids. Jeshua sat up quickly and rubbed the sleep from his weary eyes as Amar rolled to the cold ground, uttering some guttural sound that only sheep can proffer. Both the young shepherd and the tiny lamb gazed at a large, bright star that danced stately over the small bustling town of Bethlehem. Its radiance overshadowed all of the other heavenly lights and the rays of that celestial body extended to the very boundaries of Bethlehem touching a small rooftop in the heart of the walled city.

Awestricken by the lustrous light of the star, Jeshua jumped to his feet and ran to his brothers, who were huddled together, looking with wonder at this inexplicable, heavenly sign. Amar loped along behind Jeshua, his big brown eyes fixed on the night light.

"What do you make of it?" Jeshua asked. "I do not know," answered his oldest brother, "but it is brighter than any star I have ever seen, and I have spent many nights on these grassy knolls of Bethlehem." Perplexed by this mystery, the shepherd family stood silently together, staring at this nocturnal light. Amar, standing at the feet of Jeshua, moved not a muscle, for he too sensed that the star was special.

Suddenly, a strange noise interrupted the silence and sanctity of the moment; it was a muffled, rumbling sound which the surprised shepherds could not identify. "What was that noise?" Jeshua inquired. Amar looked longingly up at his curious companion. "I do not know," answered one of his brothers. "It sounded like thunder, but there is not a cloud in the sky."

Once again the rumbling resumed, but this time with clarity. It was a voice—a voice ringing out in the heavens— "Do not be afraid. I am a messenger from God." Chill bumps quickly rose on Jeshua's neck and Amar sprang into the arms of his friend, his tiny body shaking all over. Humans, as well as animals, quake at the sight of the holy—the very angel of God.

"Fear not," said the voice, "for behold I bring you good tidings of great joy which shall be to all people; for to you is born this day in the city of David, a Savior who is Christ the Lord. And this shall be a sign to you; you will find the babe wrapped in swaddling clothes, lying in a manger."

Suddenly the surrounding hills came alive with angelic music, a multitude of the heavenly hosts singing their adoring songs to the Lord; "Glory to God in the highest, and on earth, peace, goodwill toward men."

The shepherds, including Jeshua, hid their faces in fear. But Jeshua, at the prompting of Amar's nose against his neck, lifted his head momentarily to catch a glimpse of these nocturnal, celestial visitors. Only a blinding light was visible, the glory of the Almighty God of Israel.

Moments later Jeshua attempted to describe the sight that he had witnessed as Amar looked up at him approvingly. "I cannot put into human words the appearance of those angels," he said. "All I know is that heaven was with us, sharing the good news of joy with a sorrowful and burdened world."

When Jeshua and his brothers had regained their composure, they sought to understand what had happened to them in the celestial visitation. Soon they realized that a person can never understand the gracious presence of God. One can only respond to it.

So with haste, the starry-eyed shepherds traveled to Bethlehem to see if they could find that which the angel announced—a babe wrapped in swaddling clothes, lying in a manger.

Jeshua did not think twice about leaving Amar with the rest of the sheep as he and his brothers made their trek to the City of David. He cradled the small lamb against his chest as he ran to keep up with his older brothers. Amar, peering over Jeshua's elbow, had a look of contentment on his innocent, woolly face—almost smiling. Truly he and Jeshua were inseparable, even during heaven's visitation to earth.

The sound of running feet and the pounding of his young heart could not drown the voice of his mother—a voice which often spoke around the hearth at home during evening devotions: "A star shall come forth out of Jacob and a Scepter shall rise out of Israel." Yes, this was the star which Jeshua's mother had longed to see. The Lord had fulfilled his promise "For unto us a child is born, unto us a Son is given."

The star's brilliant rays reached out as if to beckon the shepherd family to a small grotto which had been hewn out of Bethlehem granite to form a simple stable. As Jeshua approached the entrance of the cave-like barn, his heart fluttered with excitement. Prophets of old had not lived to see what Jeshua was about to witness—the Messiah of Israel, the Christ of God, the Savior of the world—God's own Son.

Standing in the threshold, Jeshua and his brothers paused in silence, hoping that they were not intruding. Amar, still cradled in Jeshua's arms looked on at the silent scene as if he, too, were human.

A lump came into Jeshua's throat, and a tear seemed to trickle down Amar's fuzzy face as they peered into the face of the Christ Child. Truly it was a holy moment for this child shepherd and his lamb.

At each end of the make-shift cradle, the child's parents knelt. Briefly the man looked up and quietly motioned for the adoring shepherds to come in. The baby's mother did not utter a sound, but she acknowledged their presence with a gentle smile. She kept busy at her task of tilting the manger in a rocking fashion, while quietly humming to her newborn infant.

In one corner of the cave, several cattle chewed their cud lazily, and in another corner an awkward donkey gazed contentedly at the strange sights. How ironic! The Son of God came into the world, only to be greeted by a few clumsy animals and a handful of starry-eyed shepherds, accompanied by an almost-human lamb.

Slowly and silently, Jeshua and Amar moved toward the manger and knelt between the man and the woman. Amar looked up at Jeshua and then down at the baby and offered a soft bleating cry.

Jeshua's brothers joined him and Amar around the manger, and in silence, all marveled at the beauty of this child, and together they appeared to thank God for revealing to them this holy moment. Never in his brief life had Jeshua seen such a picturesque sight; God in a manger! It almost sounded as ridiculous as God on a cross. It was Jeshua's hope that the prophet's words about this babe would drown in the sea of forgetfulness: "He came to his own and his own received him not."

The Child's mother, Mary, was moved by the sight of a shepherd boy and his lamb kneeling at the cradle of the Babe of Bethlehem. Looking into Jeshua's eyes, Mary inquired, "What is your name?" The boy answered softly, "Jeshua." "That is the name of my child," Mary said, as she winked at the smallest shepherd. For those of us whose Hebrew might have grown a little rusty, Jeshua is a derivative of Joshua. In English, it is often shortened to Jesus, which means, "He will save."

Mary, somewhat taken with the kind face of this young boy who clutched his pet lamb close to his chest, asked a second question, "What is the name of your lamb?" "Oh, I call him Amar. It is not a very creative name, but he is so woolly and warm, that no other name will do. I saved him from a wolf that killed his mother."

How interesting, pondered Mary. Jeshua, the shepherd, saved Amar. Jeshua, the babe of the manger, will save all the lambs of his flock. For the prophet has written; "Behold the Lord will come with a strong hand. He shall feed his flock like a shepherd, he shall gather the lambs with his arm and carry them in his bosom." like Jeshua carried Amar.

Suddenly in the holy moment of adoration, a thought came to Jeshua's mind that both thrilled and frightened his soul. He must offer the newborn King a present—yet Jeshua was a peasant. All that Jeshua had to offer was literally all that he had—Amar—his closest companion, his friend and confidant, his very life.

Slowly Jeshua lifted Amar higher in his arms and whispered into his ear, explaining to the young lamb what he must do. Amar's eyes glistened with what appeared to be tears—so did Jeshua's. However, the shepherd boy knew that Amar must belong to the newborn Jeshua, the true Shepherd King.

So Jeshua, with Mary's approval, placed the tiny lamb named "Amar," next to the child called "Christ" in the cradle. Jeshua hugged Amar one last time while whispering into his ear these words: "Keep your nose on the infant's neck so that your breath will keep his tiny face warm. Lie in his bosom and cover his small body with your woolly fleece. The night air is cold. His name is Jeshua, also, and Amar, you must now be one of his lambs."

Jeshua kissed Amar on his head and held his floppy ears, oh so gently. Then the shepherd boy walked away from the manger without looking back, for sometimes it hurts to give God your best, but truly it must have hurt God to give us His best.

Fondly, Mary watched the tiny lamb lying in the bosom of her babe. His fleece truly was warmer than the swaddling clothes. She was moved by the shepherd's sacrificial gift—more precious than gold, frankincense and myrrh.

Suddenly the babe smiled as Amar's floppy ears brushed against his tiny face. Amar's ears perked up as if the child were whispering something in his ear. One never understands the mystery of the Almighty who becomes incarnate in the flesh of a baby. But Amar apparently understood, albeit no word was spoken from the child's lips.

The lamb jumped gently from the cradle and walked away. When Amar reached the stable door, he turned and looked at Joseph, then at Mary—and then one last glance at young Jeshua—the Shepherd King who gathers all lambs in his arms and carries them gently in his bosom.

Amar pranced gingerly in the chill of the night air, down the cobbled streets of Bethlehem, out of the gates of the city, on to the grassy knolls of the plains, in search of the shepherd's campfire and the strong arms of his friend, Jeshua.

In the shadowy valley between two hills, a wolf stalked the young lamb. Fear came over Amar's helpless, tiny body—that which happened to his mother was now about to happen to him.

Back in Bethlehem at that very moment, Mary noticed the movement of her babe, as if he were speaking into the night, yet without uttering a sound.

Amar stood still as the wolf moved ever so cautiously toward his tender body. Suddenly a great calm came over the anxious lamb, and Amar pranced confidently toward his predator. Their noses met as they sniffed each other's scent, and then the wolf nudged Amar on, as if to send him on his way to the safety of Jeshua's arms.

How strange that a wolf would treat a lamb so gently, but the prophet has spoken about the new era that the birth of the holy child brings: "The wolf also shall dwell with the lamb, and the leopard shall lie down with the kid; and a little child shall lead them."

As Amar walked over the crest of the last hill, he spied the shepherd's campfire; he smelled the smoke which rose heavenward like sweet perfume for angels; and he ran wildly and exuberantly toward Jeshua, the boy shepherd.

When Jeshua heard the sound of Amar's excited bleating, he ran tirelessly toward his floppy-eared, woolly friend. As they met, the tiny lamb leapt into Jeshua's arms. Amar's nose was tucked away in the nape of Jeshua's neck and the lamb's soothing breath warmed his cold face. Amar's curly fleece warmed Jeshua's chest, and the two friends embraced for what seemed like an eternity. Jeshua whispered in Amar's ear, "I love you my dear friend," and Amar offered three soft bleats, which in sheep talk means, "I love you too."

As they lay together on the cold damp ground of Bethlehem's plain, warmed by the crackling embers of the campfire and by each other's breath, both human and creature pondered the meaning of the night as dawn broke forth into a new day.

Jeshua realized that the sacrificial gift given to the Christ Child is always ten-fold and even more. Amar seemed to realize that life can only be lived in the strong arms of a shepherd, who is a constant companion and devoted friend. And this author realizes that you and I are like Amar, helpless sheep who must cling to our Jeshua, Jesus the Shepherd King, who feeds his flock like a shepherd, who gathers his lambs unto his arms and carries them safely in his bosom. And interestingly enough this Jeshua, this Babe of Bethlehem is none other than Amar, the lamb who walks away from the cradle and the crown of heaven into the wilderness as our own scapegoat, carrying our sin and death in his body, because he is the Lamb of God, who takes away the sin of the world.

As you travel to Bethlehem this year, may you find the Christ who is both shepherd and lamb, and may your relationship with him be as strong as that of Jeshua and Amar. All who find refuge in the strong arms of the shepherd, and all who are covered by the pure wool of the Lamb of God will discover and know a joyous and holy Christmas.

Christmas 2005

None is able to say it any better than Luke: "And it came to pass in those days, that there went out a decree from Caesar Augustus that all the world should be taxed."

These ancient words never get old, do they? As we read them during these Holy days, we can see—hear—and even smell the events which the beloved physician describes for us.

"And it came to pass in those days." What days? The days of Pax Romano, the peace of Rome. The Empire extended from East to West. The borders were secure. The highway system was matchless.

However, to enjoy the Pax Romano, one had to pay the price. Peace does not come without sacrifice. Armaments, war horses and troops are costly. Citizens of Rome and conquered people as well must pay taxes in order to ensure the Pax Romano throughout the Empire.

"And it came to pass in those days," that heralds were sent forth throughout the lands with an official document, stating that all the world was to be taxed in order to preserve peace and prosperity. On the final page of the decree, all saw the signature of the Emperor, and above the royal signature, they observed an etching of Caesar Augustus with his toothy, imperial smile, somehow deluded by the name he chose for himself, Augustus, the August one, the Divine King—God Himself.

Little did Caesar know that his tax decree would enable a challenger to come forth to contest his self-proclaimed divinity, one whom the prophets foretold as the true king and ruler of all.

> For unto us a child is born, unto us a son is given; and the government shall be upon His shoulders. And His name shall be called Wonderful, Counselor, The Mighty God, The Everlasting Father, the Prince of Peace.
>
> Of the increase of his government and peace there shall be no end.

Caesar Augustus can sign all the decrees in the world, edicts that proclaim his divinity and power, but he is destined as is the entire empire to kneel before the One who is the true Prince of Peace, even Jesus of Nazareth, the Savior sent from Heaven, the Mighty God, the Everlasting Father, "Who pays our taxes in His Kingdom through the price of His own blood."

The story, according to Luke, continues:

> And all went to be taxed, everyone into his own city. And

Joseph went up from Galilee, out of the city of Nazareth, into Judea, unto the city of David which is called Bethlehem because he was of the house and lineage of David to be taxed with Mary his espoused wife, being great with child.

Joseph went up from Galilee? Galilee is in the North and Bethlehem is South. Should not Luke say, Joseph went down from Galilee? Bethlehem is only a few miles from Jerusalem, the holy city, and if a pilgrim were to come from the North or East or West, he or she would be going up to God's city. A visitor always goes up when traveling toward Jerusalem and toward the holy.

So Joseph and Mary, in response to the imperial decree, make their journey to Bethlehem, some 90 miles distance. A traveler would hope to average 25 miles a day walking, so the normal time it would take to walk from Nazareth to Bethlehem would be about three and a half days.

But, Mary, great with child, would have to rest often, and so it may have taken this couple whom God has chosen to rear His child, as many as six or seven days to arrive in Bethlehem.

More than likely, they started out from Nazareth in a caravan, but as time passed, their fellow sojourners left them behind and the holy couple traveled alone. Mary, ostensibly, rides on the back of a donkey as Joseph leads the humble beast over the rocky, and at times dangerous paths.

We see the tender scene as Joseph starts and stops often, lifting

Mary down and up as she tries to find comfort from her comfortless station in life. Mary groans often as the labor pains increase, and the donkey picks up the pace, at Joseph's urging, while the "clop, clop" sound of donkey hooves can be heard keenly in the stillness of evening.

The Prince of Peace rides a donkey, as it were, to his birth and, ironically, thirty-three years later he rides a donkey to his death. The humble beast announces the advent and the reign of the Prince of Peace.

Finally, the couple arrives in Bethlehem, that town to which the prophets pointed:

> And thou Bethlehem in the land of Judah art not the least among the princes of Judah, for out of Thee shall come forth a Governor that shall rule my people Israel.

The word Bethlehem comes from two Hebrew words, *beth* which means house, and *lehan* which means bread. Bethlehem, the house of bread, is the birthplace of the one who said, "I am the bread of Life."

The governor who comes forth from Bethlehem rules the world with truth and grace and makes the nations sing because he saves his people from their sins

The Bread of Life is born in the house of bread. The smell of fresh baked bread permeates the streets of Bethlehem. The headiness of wine wafts through the still, night air. The sound of laughter waxes and wanes as one after another gives his assessment of Caesar's tax plan. And Joseph, on behalf of his pregnant wife, knocks on door after door of all the inns in Bethlehem only to be turned away with the same frightening response, "No room at the inn."

Although Luke does not tell us, we can only assume that there was a kind and compassionate innkeeper who pointed Joseph to a stable where he and Mary could lodge, while waiting for the birth of their baby.

> And so it was that while they were there, the days were accomplished that she should be delivered. And she brought forth her firstborn son and wrapped him in swaddling clothes and laid him in a manger because there was no room in the inn.

The stable becomes the delivery room. There is no smell of antiseptic, just the scent of fresh straw upon which Mary lies. With one final push, she screams in pain as the baby Jesus leaps forth from the womb of humanity as heaven and earth become one, as humanity and divinity are joined. There he is, so small, so tiny, so delicate. A baby, God's baby, lying in a manger bed of hay. His smooth infant flesh feels like expensive velvet. Do we dare kneel before his holy bed? Do we dare touch the flesh of God? The Flesh of God, God incarnate in the humanity of a baby.

As John says:

> And the Word became flesh and dwelt among us, and we beheld His glory.
>
> And there were in the same country shepherds, abiding in their fields, keeping watch over their flocks by night... And

lo, the angel of the Lord came upon them and the Glory of the Lord shone round about them and they were sore afraid.

Which one of us would not be afraid? Fear grasps the unholy when humanity stands before the holiness of God and His Kingdom. Simple shepherds shake and quake and fall face to the ground at Heaven's holy visitation. They were sore afraid. And the angel of the Lord said to them, "Fear not." Humans are filled with fear when they kneel before that which is holy.

But Heaven always allays our fears with the inevitable. Fear not. Do not be afraid. What is it other than the angel's presence that causes fear to cease? Heaven's announcement lifts the fearful to their feet.

Fear not, for behold I bring you good tidings of great joy, which shall be to all people. For unto you is born this day in the city of David, a Savior which is Christ the Lord.

And this shall be a sign unto you: Ye shall find the babe wrapped in swaddling clothes, lying in a manger. And suddenly there was with the angel a multitude of the heavenly host praising God and saying, "Glory to God in the highest, and on earth, peace, goodwill to all."

Someone had to announce the birth of heaven's child. Mary cannot. She is tired and in repose. Joseph cannot. He refuses to leave Mary's side. The dumb beast of the stable cannot. They can only utter deep guttural moans at that which they witnessed, the birth of God, the joining of the mortal and immortal. The sleeping citizens of Bethlehem cannot for in their sleep, they know not the glorious event.

So heaven announces to earth the good tidings of great joy, and the speaker of heaven is none other than Gabriel, the angel of the Lord. "For unto you is born this day in the city of David a savior which is Christ, the Lord."

This is not the message of Pax Romana which is announced nor is it to Caesar Augustus that the announcement is made. Rather, it is the message of Peace, the Peace of salvation which the Savior brings to us because He saves us from our sins.

The message is first announced to lowly shepherds who were considered by many to be the lowest of the lowest—dishonest, disreputable sinners through and through. Thus, the angel's message, the gospel of grace and forgiveness is given first of all to those who sin and know their great need for mercy.

For unto you is born this day in the city of David a Savior which is Christ the Lord.

That is the message which comes through cloven skies. It is the message that comes through cloudy skies of this day. It is the message of heaven to you and me during these holy days. Hear it again:

> For unto you is born this day in the city of David a Savior which is Christ the Lord.

A Savior!

> And it came to pass, as the angels were gone away from them into heaven, the shepherds said one to another, 'Let us now go even unto Bethlehem and see this thing which

is come to pass which the Lord has made known unto us.' And they came with haste.

With the gift of peace, the gift of grace granted by our Savior, God demands a response, a response filled with haste, a response of giving ourselves to the Savior whom we adore and serve.

When Isaiah saw the Lord, high and lifted up, he heard the Lord speak, "Whom shall I send and who will go for us?" And then he said to the Holy, "Here am I, send me."

Christmas is responding to a baby, to the birth of a baby, to God's baby whom we proclaim as Lord and Savior. And we whisper to Him whose face shines with Infant Light: "Here am I, Your obedient servant. Send me."

"And they came with haste and found Mary and Joseph and the babe lying in a manger." And they knelt in adoration. The story comes to a conclusion with the shepherd folk. The sights and sounds are heartwarming in this story.

But we must not ignore the scent of the stable and those who have spent time in barns know what I mean. There is the delightful smell of corn and oats, and hay and straw, a pleasing aroma that is challenged by the scent of animal waste, that wretched smell that somehow symbolizes our human plight.

Warfare seeks to overcome peace. Evil seeks to overshadow the good. Pain persists over pleasure. Temptation tries to lure us away and death dangles its ugly head in our grieving hearts. Life is too often like the displeasing scent of the stable, a scent which permeates our human fiber.

However, it is into the stable with all of its pleasing and displeasing scents that Christ is born. His birth occurs in the midst of life and in all of its contradictions. And Heaven says to our troubled hearts: "Fear not, For behold I bring you good tidings of great joy which shall be to all people [in all situations]. For unto you is born this day in the city of David, a Savior which is Christ the Lord."

And we respond to any and to all angelic news with the human words: "Yea though I walk through the valley of deep gloom, through the valley of tainted straw, I will fear no evil. For thou art with me, with me in the beautiful, soft flesh of an infant. Even Jesus our Savior, to whom belongs glory, dominion, and power—now and always."

A Transfiguration Day Sermon

The closest I have ever been to Rome is Athens, Greece, and I envy those of you who have had the privilege of walking the streets of that ancient city. I hope to get there one day, and my first stop after the Coliseum will be the Sistine Chapel to view that marvelous work of Michelangelo.

The philosopher William Irwin Thompson tells about his experience in the Sistine Chapel. Upon entering that marvelous structure, he says, the painting did not look all that impressive. People chattered and joked about a paint-by-number replica of Michelangelo's work for their own ceilings. But when the crowd drew closer, they were overwhelmed. The painting seemed to engulf them, and everyone became quiet. Necks ached with the effort to keep looking up and the impact of the paintings message was unforgettable.

Then Thompson says in his journal, that he noticed a fly crawling across the paintings, and be thought, "What a shame. That fly is right up there where I would love to be. He is right on top of it—but he just can't see it."

Dr. Thompson then penned these famous lines: "In life we are like flies crawling across the ceiling of the Sistine Chapel. We cannot see what angels and gods lie underneath the threshold of our perceptions."

The Gospel for this last Sunday in Epiphany is always the account of the transfiguration. Luke, like the others, presents this miraculous occurrence in a series of magnificent paintings.

In the first painting, like the remaining, the setting is a mountain-top. None of the Gospels identifies the exact location. One tradition says Mt. Tabor; another says Mt. Hermon. However, we know that Jesus is still near Caesarea Philippi and there is too great a distance to have been the sight of the transfiguration. Thus one can say it was one of the highest points near Caesarea Philippi. In this first painting. Luke reveals Jesus with the inner circle of disciples: Peter, James and John. Jesus is praying and Luke interjects a bit of humor—the disciples are sleeping. That is, they knew that Jesus often prayed all night and so they slept like I use to do when my boyhood pastor prayed for twenty minutes each Sunday during the pastoral prayer. If one sleeps twenty minutes during the prayer and twenty-five minutes during the sermon, he/she can catch a good catnap and the disciples napped, not knowing what they were missing just like they did not know what they were missing in Gethsemane when they slept through our Lord's praying prior to his arrest.

In the second painting, one sees the results of Jesus' prayer. The appearance of our Lord's face is changed, and his clothes are as bright as a flash of lightning. This transfiguration was a transaction between the Father and His beloved Son incarnate, who always received everything from the Father. Matthew says that our Lord's countenance "shone like the sun." Mark says of the whiteness: "such as a fuller on earth is not able to whiten." But Luke says, "It was dazzling white like the flashing of lightning.

Peter later stated in his second epistle, "We were eyewitnesses to his majesty." John refers to it when he wrote the Revelation: "The Lamb sits in the midst of the heavenly city and He is the Light therein." In this second painting we see that Jesus, once he is transfigured, is visited by two citizens from the heavenly realm: Moses and Elijah. Moses was the great representative of the Law and Elijah the great representative of Prophecy. The appearance of these two from heaven above was to assure the disciples that the death of their Master was in perfect accord with the Old Testament prophecies concerning the Messiah.

Luke alone records the subject of conversation betwixt Jesus and the heavenly visitors: "His departure which he was about to accomplish in Jerusalem." The interesting Greek word that Luke employs in this heavenly conversation is *Esodos*, whence comes our word Exodus, meaning the road out.

The conversation of Jesus, Moses and Elijah shows the disciples that Jesus is about to depart on an Exodus by which he will leave this earth for the heavenly realm by way of the cross, resurrection and ascension. And all the saints in heaven looked forward to the accomplishment of Jesus.

Peter and the others, once asleep are now fully awake, and impetuous Peter says to Jesus, "Master it is good for us to be here. Let us put up three shelters—one for you, one for Moses and one for Elijah. Luke informs us that Peter, dazzled by the sight, does not know what he is saying.

The one thing that has always troubled me at this point in the paintings is this: How did the disciples know that these two were Elijah and Moses? Obviously they had never seen them and the gospels do not tell us that Jesus introduces them. One can only surmise that the saints in heaven need not be introduced and named to us but are known at once through an intuition that is always wrought by God.

Nonetheless, it was Peter's desire to prolong and preserve this mountaintop experience and when they came into our lives, we too opt for staying in the heights rather than returning to the depths of life.

In the third painting a cloud appeared and enveloped these disciples. Matthew tells us the cloud was white, signifying the loving presence of God as the pillar of cloud and fire had done for these departing on the first Exodus. When one is in the presence of God, grace prevails. God always speaks. "This is my Son, whom I have chosen; listen to Him." It was the same voice that spoke at our Lord's baptism. It is the Lord God's voice that confirms that Jesus is still the Father's Elect who was chosen to do His great work redeeming the world which He will accomplish in the cross and resurrection. For those of us who fear the present and or the future—God comes in His grace and says look and listen.

In the final painting the voice of the Father is now silent. The cloud has departed. Jesus and the three disciples are alone once more. Luke implies that there is a strange and mysterious look on the faces of the disciples, and the gospel tells us they "kept this to themselves and told no one at the time what they had seen."

On this final Sunday of Epiphany as we move toward Ash Wednesday, how shall we deal with the four memorable paintings from the Mount of Transfiguration? Shall we observe them briefly and marvel at the hand of the artist and then move on to other notable paintings with no thought of what the artist is trying to say? Worse yet, shall we become like flies on the ceiling of the Sistine Chapel who see such works of art as momentary resting places, but have no powers to discern their ultimate worth? Or shall we look for some deeper meaning, some relevant truth about our own lives and destinies?

The first thing that these paintings seem to say to us is there is more to reality than what you and I can hear, see, touch, taste, or smell.

Do you remember the German classic Faust? Goethe describes a pact that Dr. Faust makes with the devil. The pact allows Faust to satisfy his very human want and desire except one. Never, never under any circumstances is his ever to stop and say to the passing moment, "Wait, you are so beautiful."

The seasons are changing before our eyes even this day. All about us we see beautiful sights and beautiful human beings. This world is mystical, magical and magnificent, overwhelming our senses as we contemplate the glory of creation, which is ours.

The Mount of Transfiguration says to you and me something very clear. When we take the sum total of every beautiful and wonderful thing that we have ever experienced through our five senses; when we add up every good feeling we have ever had about family, friends, health and hope; when we include everything this world has to offer us for happiness, there is still more. There is a reality that science cannot measure and philosophy cannot fathom. It is the realm of the spiritual, the realm of the heavenly, the reality of the living and loving God where the saints cheer us on, and Jesus, our Advocate prays for us. It is the reality in which you and I live and the reality in which you and I long to live forever.

The second statement that these paintings seem to say to us is that there is more to living than dying.

Several months ago I saw an article in *Time Magizine* about all the mail that comes in to the White House—60,000 pieces of mail a week. President Bush received a strange letter, inviting him to the funeral of a man described as a hard-working, patriotic American. The man, however, was not dead. In the letter to the President, the family explained that he was hooked to a life-support machine and the family could pull the plug to suit Mr. Bush's schedule. Death on demand. Death with dignity. Code words in this modern era. For us Christians, however, there is a more pressing issue. Death's domain is defeated.

There on the Mount of Transfiguration, the disciples see Jesus and Moses and Elijah. Moses was buried with God's own hand. Elijah was taken up into heaven without dying. How long had these two been with God? A thousand years? Five hundred years? It does not matter, for in the heavenly realm there is no measure of time, for the scriptures say, "With God a thousand years is a day." Jesus proclaimed, "God is a God of the living." Death is reality, but a reality that moves us from the realm below to the realm above setting us free to live life to the fullest. Who can doubt such grace? Who can fear such wonder? Who can doubt such truth?

Mayo Mathers tells the story of his son whose best friend Luke died at age eleven of a brain hemorrhage. It is a warm story of a young boy who grieves and of an insightful mother who helps her child through that grief.

She suggested that her son write Luke a letter, telling him how much he missed him and loved him and that he hadn't forgotten him. Hopefully, she thought this would help her son work through his feelings of loss.

The boy followed his mother's instructions and wrote a letter of love—a message from earth to heaven.

Then the boy said to his mother, "What I really want to do is tie my letter to a balloon. I know it can't really get to heaven, but…" leaving the sentence unfinished.

So she drove him to the store where they purchased a helium balloon. They made their way to the high desert mountains. And the boy released the balloon and the letter tied to it. It instantly danced away from his fingers. Up, up, up it climbed as if it knew the importance of the mission.

The boy looking toward the heavens said to his mother, "I wish something would happen so I could know God got the letter."

"I do too," said his mother, yet her practical side spoke, assuring her so that God would give Luke the message regardless of what happened to the balloon.

The sky was covered with thick, heavy clouds and the balloon grew smaller and smaller. Then suddenly just as the balloon was leaving their vision, an opening appeared in the clouds, and the balloon sailed through. Mother and Son stood speechless and then the boy whispered reverently: "Did you see that, Mom? God got my balloon."

The boy and his mother must have felt what Peter, James and John felt as the could enveloped them on the Mount of Transfiguration. There is more to life than our human senses can detect and there is a blessed life beyond death.

I conclude with this final thought from the gospel paintings as it were. There is more to our Christian life than going to the mountain top.

There should be a fifth painting of the Transfiguration. Luke adds it but he does not include it as a part of the experience. The fifth painting would show Jesus and the three disciples going down the mountain ministering to the great needs of the people.

Peter suggested that they build the tabernacles and stay on the blissful mountain, but, says Luke, he didn't know what he was saying.

God gives us in life rich realities, eerie experiences of the spiritual realm, assuring us of His strong gracious presence and of the certainty of life eternal. However this grace is granted so that we will not sit by and twiddle our thumbs in luxury, idly reveling in these great truths. We are sent down from the lofty heights to the depressing depths of earth where we seek out the least and lowliest who suffer in the great struggles of this life.

The test of every mountaintop experience with the living Christ is this: Does it motivate us to reach out to our neighbor? Does it motivate us to become involved in the painful struggles of humanity? There is no staying on the mountain top 'til life in this realm ends, for the transfigured and risen Christ leads us down the mountain into the valley where His work with people is accomplished.

What about you and me? How do we feel about these paintings of the Transfiguration that Luke has given us? Are we like the critic who views them with detachment and then moves on? Are we like the fly on the ceiling of the Sistine Chapel with no awareness there is anything great here. Or does the awe that we experience in the mighty unseen realities of God's Kingdom, push us toward that which is seen—the fields that are ripe for harvest, the suffering of God's children in the valley below, suffering that awaits the healing of God through the gifts that He has given to us?

Prayer

How good it is to be with You, O Christ of God, glorified in human flesh. Yet we know that we cannot remain with You on the lofty heights for You bid us to leave the mountain. Come with us to the plain where the cries of people can be heard. Amen.

Unity in the Church
John 17:1-26
Ephesians 4:1-6

Only in John's Gospel do we find "the High Priestly Prayer" of the Savior. Between the Prologue and the accounts of the three post-resurrection appearances—all of which are unique to the Gospel of St. John—one finds this magnificent prayer for the church.

In the preceding chapters one discovers events and teachings which the synoptics fail to mention—events and teachings that somehow confirm who Jesus is and why he prays for the church.

John reveals, as no other, the Lord's first miracle of turning water into wine at the wedding at Cana in Galilee. John says, "There he revealed his glory, and his disciples believed in him."

Next, the reader encounters the exchange between Jesus and Nicodemus, who came to our Lord under the cover of night. The Savior spoke these unique words to the inquisitive Pharisee: "No one can see the Kingdom of God unless he is born again."

On his way to Galilee, Jesus has a conversation with a woman from Samaria, and in the course of this conversation, Jesus speaks these words to the woman, who has come to draw water from the well: "Whoever drinks this water will thirst again; but whoever drinks the water that I will give him will never thirst again."

At a religious festival in Jerusalem, Jesus approaches the pool at Bethesda where he sees a lame man who had lived with this infirmity for thirty-eight years. Jesus approached him and said, "Do you want to get well?" Then the Savior said, "Pick up your mat and walk."

Who can forget that marvelous account of the woman caught in adultery? Prepared to stone her to death, the officials asked Jesus, what does the law require? Our Lord answered, "He who is without sin, cast the first stone."

At Bethany, Jesus is revealed by John as the one who can raise the dead. Jesus spoke these hopeful words to Martha, sister of the dead man Lazarus: "I am the resurrection and the life. Whosoever believes in me will live even though he/she dies; and who lives and believes in me will never die."

Then Jesus speaks in a loud voice: "Lazarus, Come Forth!" And the dead man walked out of the tomb. Jesus said, "Unbind him and let him go."

John also shows us a unique experience—the washing of the disciples' feet by Jesus in the upper room. In the synoptics, the institution of the Lord's Supper takes precedence over all that happens in that Passover meal. However, in John's Gospel, the central theme in the upper room is our Lord's servanthood, as he kneels to wash the feet of his followers.

Jesus speaks: "You call me Teacher and Lord, and it is right that you do so, because that is what I am. I, your Lord and Teacher, have just washed your feet. You, then should wash one another's feet."

As the evening passed, Jesus gave a new commandment to his disciples: "Love one another. As I have loved you, so you must love one another. If you have love for one another, then everyone will know that you are my disciples."

Then our Lord spoke words of comfort to his disciples and to believers of all ages: "Let not your hearts be troubled, neither let them be afraid. Believe in God, believe also in me. In my Father's house are many rooms. If it were not so, I would have told you. But I go to prepare a place for you and if I go to prepare a place for you, I will come again and take you unto myself that where I am, you may be also."

Only John helps us to see and to hear Jesus' legacy: "Peace I leave with you, my peace I give unto you. Not as the world giveth, give I unto you. Let not your hearts be troubled—neither let them be afraid."

On the heels of our Lord's legacy, we see, thanks to John, Jesus' "High Priestly Prayer." The events in the upper room come to a conclusion with this prayer, in which Jesus prays for himself, for his disciples, and for the Church which the Spirit will call into existence at Pentecost.

In the first petition, our Savior prays: "Father, the hour has come. Give glory to Your Son, so that the Son may glorify You. For you gave him authority over all humankind; so that he might give eternal life to all those you gave him."

"And eternal life means to know you, the only true God, and to know Jesus Christ."

Jesus says that the hour of his death has come. The Savior accepts that impending death—and in the glorious resurrection, the Father will glorify the Son, and the Son will glorify the Father.

Then, our Lord defines eternal life; "Eternal life is to know the Father as the only true God and Jesus Christ as His son, who has been sent to carry out God's divine purpose." This is eternal life: To know God through Jesus Christ, our Savior.

Previous to the High Priestly Prayer, Jesus speaks about eternal life. In the third chapter, we discover once again those words which bring peace: "For God so loved the world that He gave his only begotten Son, that whosoever believes in Him will not perish, but have everlasting eternal life.

In the fifth chapter we hear these words of the Savior: "Whoever hears my words and believes Him who sent me has eternal life. He will not be judged, but has already passed from death to life."

Do we hear the words of the Savior? The Church holds within its grasp the richest of pearls—the message of the Savior—the promise of eternal life.

In the second petition of Jesus' prayer, our Lord prays for his disciples: "Father I am coming to you, and I say these things in the world so that they might have my joy in their hearts—in all of its fullness. I gave them your message and the world hated them . . . I do not ask you to take them out of the world, but I do ask you to keep them safe from the Evil One . . . Dedicate them to your truth."

Pilate asked Jesus, "What is Truth?" Jesus stood silently before Pilate and said nothing. Truth is Jesus Christ.

"Dedicate them to your truth," Jesus prays. What is truth? Jesus defines it this way: "I tell you this before it happens; so that when it does happen you will believe that I Am Who I Am!" Jesus Christ is Truth—The Very Son of God.

Now comes the meat of the prayer—at least for us. It is the third petition: "I pray for those who believe in me because of their message. I pray that they may be one . . . so that the world will believe that you sent me . . . may they be one just as you and I are one."

Here is the message of John's Gospel. All the unique events in Jesus' life and ministry, which only John reveals, point to this truth: The Son and the Father are One. Prior to this prayer, Jesus speaks: I Am Who I Am.

So our Lord prays for His Church—and that for which He prays is for the Unity of the Church—a unity as close as that which exists between the Father and the Son. Then—and only then—will the world believe that the Father has sent the Son—our Savior—and that this gospel is true.

It seems to me that Jesus is saying very frankly that if the world is to believe in the Son of God, the world must experience the Unity of the Church: "May they be One so that the world will believe that you sent me."

Unity in the Church is the prayer of Jesus. Unity in the Church is the will of God. As the psalmist says, "Behold how good and how pleasant it is for brothers and sisters to dwell in unity."

William Sloane Coffin, who recently entered the Church Triumphant, has written these words in his book *Credo*: "A Church is a place where we try to think, and act in God's way—not in the way of a fear-filled world."

"A Church is a home for love, a home for us to dwell in unity—to rest and be healed, to let go of our defenses and be free—free from worry—free to laugh."

From his prison cell, Paul writes to the Ephesians: "I urge you, then—I who am a prisoner because I serve the Lord—Live a life that measures up to the standard God set when he called you: Be always humble, gentle and patient. Show your love by being tolerant with one another. Do your best to preserve the unity which the Spirit gives by means of the peace that binds you together."

And then Paul lists those realities which unify us: "There is one body and one spirit, just as there is one hope to which God has called you. There is one Lord, one faith, one baptism. There is one God and Father of all, who is Lord of all, works through all and in you all."

Paul emphasizes this truth: It is the Holy Spirit who gives unity through the bonds of peace. It is the legacy: "Peace I leave with you; my peace I give to you . . . let not your hearts be troubled." Unity is a gift of the Holy Spirit, and it is received gratefully by the Church, a Church that knows its legacy.

The late Shirley C. Guthrie often spoke these words: "Where there is unity, the Holy Spirit is present; where there is disunity, the Holy Spirit is absent."

Is the Holy Spirit present or absent in the life and ministry of PCUSA? How do we experience Unity when we are so divided over conflicting issues, namely over the issue of whom we ordain? How do we respond to the burning issues before us in order that uniting, in one form or another, may exist?

Allow me briefly, to suggest three options we have as we face that which causes strife in our midst.

The first option is this: We can fight amongst ourselves.

There is a story about a famous lawyer from New York City who traveled to Tennessee to hunt ducks. The lawyer shot a duck which fell across the fence of another person's property. As the lawyer climbed the fence to retrieve the duck, the owner of the property, an aging farmer, appeared and asked the lawyer what he was doing. The lawyer said, "I shot a duck; it fell over the fence, and I'm going to get it"

"No, you are not," answered the farmer. "That's my property, and you will be trespassing."

"If you get in my way," said the attorney, "I will sue you for everything you have. I am a lawyer from New York, you know."

The old farmer looked at the attorney and said, "That's not the way we settle things in Tennessee."

"Please sir," said the lawyer, "tell me how you settle disagreements in this state?"

"We have the three kick rule."

"What is the three kick rule, inquired the frustrated lawyer."

"Well, said the farmer, I kick you three times, and then you kick me three times till one of us gives up."

The lawyer studied the stature of the farmer and said to himself, "I can beat this guy handily." So the attorney agreed to the terms of the fight.

The old farmer kicked the lawyer in the shins, and when he grabbed his shins in pain, the farmer then kicked him in the stomach; and when the lawyer fell to the ground in pain, the farmer kicked him in the head.

Dazed, the lawyer lay there trying to regain his wits; and he lay there for quite a while. When he found the strength to stand, he looked at the farmer and said, "Okay old man, it's my time to kick you."

The old farmer, with eyes gleaming and with a sly smile on his face said, "Son, I give up. You can have the duck."

The humorous story somehow represents church fights, which are devious and denigrating. Rules change and participants always experience a beating. Someone wins and someone loses. Unity and

Harmony are lost in the fray. Church fights provide an opportune time for the Evil One to work in our midst, keeping us tuned to methods of fighting instead of sharing the message of the gospel.

Fighting amongst ourselves is nothing more than the "Three kick rule." Someone is going to get hurt.

Secondly, we can express our displeasure about the theological strife in our midst by leaving, by withdrawing, by disassociating ourselves with our beloved Church. I understand that Presbyterians have been meeting and planning possible withdrawals if certain events take place at the General Assembly.

However, withdrawal does not work; division only leads to more division. In 1975, I was called as the pastor to the First Presbyterian Church in Rock Hill, South Carolina. I was twenty-seven years old at the time, and I was green with inexperience. Approximately nine hundred members left, and I was called to be the Shepherd of one hundred and forty faithful members who remained.

Unbeknownst to me, when I arrived on the scene, was the stark reality that a lawsuit had been filed to determine who was the true Church—the loyal minority or the majority. The United States Supreme Court upheld the ruling of the South Carolina State Supreme Court that the loyal minority was the "True Church."

It is embarrassing when people of faith turn to civil courts to solve their faith for them. However one experiences even more embarrassment at the deep pain families in the church experience. Not only is their church divided, but so are their families. I had husbands in one church and wives in another. Children in one church, parents in another. Brother in one church, sisters in another. There is no greater pain than to see brothers and sisters living in disunity. They can no longer worship together because pride owns them.

Believe me, you never want to find yourself in the kind of destructive situation where the Body of Christ is broken and bleeding. The pain overshadows the glory of the Gospel, and it takes a long time to recover. As long as the church "licks its wounds" as it were, the tongue is not proclaiming the Gospel. Withdrawal is not the answer! Division leads to more division.

Finally, I close with this parable that I heard Carl Dudley tell almost thirty years ago. The Apache nation gathered at the foot of the Holy Mountain when the sun, moon and stars were in a certain alignment. The gathering was to celebrate young "braves" becoming warriors. To become a warrior one had to travel into the unknown and return, before night with a gift for the Nation. With great joy, the Nation sent their young men off on their mission. And then waited for their return.

As the shadows of evening lengthened, the first brave returned with a deer around his shoulders, a deer he killed with his own hands. And all marveled.

Then came another brave carrying an herb for the healing of the Nation. And all marveled.

The people gasped as the next brave entered the camp, carrying a rare bush that grew between "life and no life." And all marveled that someone could run so far in one day.

As dusk became darkness, the final brave entered the camp, shouting, "I have seen it! I have seen it—the shimmering of the sea."

The old chief stood while raising his hands above his head and asked the Nation this question: Which can we live without? Good? Healing? Human accomplishment? Or vision?

I submit to you that our Presbytery and our General Assembly can live without food, healing and human accomplishment. However, one thing we cannot live without is vision.

Vision of the one who turns water into wine, vision of Him who gives us living water; vision of Him who tells us to pick up our mat and walk; vision of the one who forgives our sin; vision of the one who says, "I am the Resurrection and the Life." Vision of the one who washes our feet and tells us to embrace servanthood; vision of one who gives us eternal life through our faith in him; vision of the one who dies in our stead, forgiving our sins; vision of the resurrected Lord standing in the garden, calling our name. Vision of the one who prays in the upper room and in all places and in all times. "Father I pray that they may be one, just as you and I are one."

Pray for us Lord Jesus! Pray that we your Church may know oneness just as the Son and the Father are one.

Prayer

Now unto Him who is able to keep you from falling,

and to present you faultless before the presence of his glory

with exceeding joy: To the only wise God our Savior,

be glory and majesty, dominion and power both now and forever.

The Word of Life
John 1: 1-5

Do you remember that chapter in Dr. Zhivago where a group dragged a young man out to the edge of town to execute him? Crying and begging for mercy, the prisoner said, "Comrades, it will never happen again. I promise. Please do not kill me. I haven't lived yet."

Have you ever felt like you haven't lived yet?

The most encompassing word in The Gospel According to John is life. In the Prologue, we read these words:

> In the beginning was the Word, and the Word was with God, and the Word was God. He was in the beginning with God. All things were made through Him, and without Him was not anything made that was made. In Him was life.

John then concludes his Gospel in this manner: "These things are written that you may believe that Jesus is the Christ, the Son of God, and that believing you may live in His name." The message of John and the message of Christmas are posed in the form of a question: Have you learned to live yet?

In his Gospel Matthew uses the word life seven times. Mark uses it only four times, and Luke mentions it five times. However, in John's Gospel we read the word life thirty-five times. Listen for some of the ways John quotes our Lord's words about life:"I am the resurrection and the life." "I am the way, the truth, and the life." "I am the light of the world; he who follows me shall not walk in darkness, but shall have the light of life."

"Simon Peter answered him, 'Lord, to whom shall we go? You have the words of eternal life.'"

"I came that they may have life, and have it abundantly."

What does John mean by this important word life? How does he understand Jesus' concept of life? As we said, John presents Jesus as the Revealer of God. He traces the resurrection of Jesus to the fact that as the Logos of God and as the Eternal Son of God. Jesus is life and has life in Himself because He is the creative power of God. As the Logos, the Eternal Christ has always had life, and He gives that life to every believing person in the creation. He was in the beginning with God. All things were made through Him and without Him was not anything made that was made. In Him was life. "I am the living bread that came down out of heaven. If anyone eats of this bread, he shall live forever."

Jesus, the Eternal Christ, created all of life, but only to human creatures does He give His life: "I came that they may have life and have it abundantly."

What is the kind of life that the Eternal Christ imparts? For John, the word life is qualitative one. It is the life that God and the Logos intended it to be in the beginning before the first man and woman sinned. John uses the word life and the words eternal life interchangeably, and shows no real preference for either expression. He uses the word life eighteen times and the word eternal life seventeen times in his Gospel. The addition of the adjective eternal does not alter his meaning of life. For example, notice the parallel construction in the following verse: "He who believes in the Son has eternal life; he who does not obey the Son shall not see life, but the wrath of God rests upon him" (John 3:36).

In the true sense of the word, only God is eternal, therefore eternal life is that life which God lives. Christmas means that Jesus came to offer us God's own life. He came to invite us to enter into the very life of God.

Eternal life obviously carries a quantitative connotation. God's life endures forever, and is repeatedly used in the Scriptures to describe God. Therefore, those who have eternal life have a certain kind of life. It is a life in fellowship with God. It is a life like God's.

As Jesus in His farewell prayer, "And this is life, that they may know Thee, the only true God, and Jesus Christ, who Thou has sent." The good news of Christmas is that the Christ Child comes in order that our life can be like that of the Father and of the Son.

How is our life like the life of God? As John says in his first epistle, "God is love, and whoever lives in love lives in union with God and God lives in union with him." God's life is a life of love: "For God so loved the world, that He gave His only begotten Son that whoever believes in Him shall not perish, but have eternal life."

For John, a person has life by living in God's life: "I am the vine, and you are the branches. Whoever remains in me and I in him will bear much fruit. My Father's glory is shown by your bearing much fruit and in this way you become my disciples. I love you just as the Father loves me; remain in my love. My commandment is this: love one another, just as I love you."

Only God is eternal, and the life He lives is eternal, i.e., it has a certain quality about it. The quality is the love. Those who are in Christ have eternal life. Their life is like God's life, full of love.

John illustrates God's eternal life of love with at least three incidents in the life of Jesus. God's love is reconciling love, and we see this reconciling love in Jesus as He reached out to the Samaritan woman at the well, offering her living water.

It was no secret that Jews disliked Samaritans. Yet, Jesus, a Jew, broke down the barrier that separated one race from another. As God broke down the barrier that separated sinful humans from Him, so Jesus broke down barriers that separated people from each other. God's reconciling love is initiating love. God did not wait for us to come to Him. He came to us.

Those who are in Christ live with reconciling love, taking the initiative to break down barriers that separate people of all races from each other. Those who do not initiate reconciliation do not want eternal life. They do not want to live like God. The life of God is a life of reconciling love.

The second incident in John's Gospel which illustrates God's eternal life of love is seen in the description of the woman caught in adultery. The Pharisees caught a woman in the act of adultery and brought her to Jesus saying, "Teacher, the Law of Moses commanded that such a woman must be stoned to death. Now, what do you say?"

John tells us that Jesus bent down and wrote on the ground with his finger. Then he straightened up and said, "Whichever of you has committed no sin may throw the first stone at her."

When the woman's accusers walked away Jesus said to her, "Where are they? Is there no one to condemn you?"

She answered, "No one, sir."

Jesus said, "I do not condemn you either. Go and sin no more."

God's eternal life of love is a forgiving love! He initiated forgiveness by sending His Son to us at Christmas.

He taught accusing, pious people that eternal life is a life of forgiveness, and that if we want to share God's life, we will live like Him, i.e., initiating reconciliation and forgiveness. How often have we sat in church, worshiping the Eternal God, while holding a grudge against someone and doing absolutely nothing about it?

The third incident in the Fourth Gospel which illustrates God's eternal life of love is found in the description of Jesus washing the disciples' feet in the Upper Room. After washing His followers' feet, Jesus said to them, "Do you understand what I have just done for you? I, your Lord and Teacher, have just washed your feet. You then should wash another's feet. I have set an example for you, so that you will do what I have just done for you."

"I am telling you the Truth: no slave is greater than his master, and no messenger is greater than the one who sent him. Now that you know this truth, how happy you will be if you put it into practice."

As the Synoptic writers tell us, Jesus said, "The Son of Man did not come to be served, but to serve." God's eternal life of love is a serving love, and those who desire to share His life will live like servants one to another. Eternal life is a certain kind of life which is committed to serving all people in the world in the name of Jesus Christ. Whom are we serving?

John is emphatic about the fact that eternal life is a certain quality of life. It is a life that is lived like God's. It is a life of reconciling, forgiving, and serving love.

Think for a moment about the positive repercussions that God's eternal life of love has for the world when we, by His grace, live our life like His.

However, one must remember that eternal life is not quantitative. The eternal life of love in Jesus Christ last forever, and even death cannot destroy it. The good news of Christmas is the good news of Easter. The resurrection of Jesus grants us the privilege of living like

God forever.

For John eternal life is not something that begins in the eschatological future. Eternal life is now in the present time.

Jesus said, "Whoever hears my words and believes in Him who sent me has eternal life. He will not be judged, but has already passed from death to life." The good news of Christmas is that you and I have eternal life now. It begins when we say, "I believe." As our Lord said, "He who believes in the Son has eternal life."

Eternal life is an experience and a reality from the moment we believe. So John encourages his readers not to place all of their hopes on the distant future when Jesus will come again, lest they fail to recognize and appreciate what is already theirs in the life of the Logos, the Eternal Christ of God.

What better Christmas gift can one receive than the assurance that eternal life is now and lasts forever? Lent frees us from the cry, "I have not lived yet. Lent frees us from the search for happiness in something in order that we may find happiness in living our life forever like that of the One who created and redeemed us.

Prayer

Jesus, Thou Joy of loving hearts, Thou Fount of life, Thou Light of men. From the best bliss that earth imparts, we turn unfilled to Thee again.

A Lenten Quest

Old Testament Lesson: Psalm 51
New Testament Lesson: John 14: 15-26

As the congregation stood to profess its faith through the words of the Apostles' Creed, a young boy listened intently to all the strange and unfamiliar words that the people around him were speaking. As they began the second and final paragraph of the magnificent creed, the youngster's eyes danced with curiosity and his mouth dropped wide open when he heard the congregation say in unison, "I believe in the Holy Ghost." He tugged furiously at his mother's sleeve, and when she leaned down to listen to her anxious son, he whispered, "I sure do hope that Holy Ghost is a friendly ghost!"

One can easily see how a young child can experience confusion as he/she hears the words. "I believe in the Holy Ghost." What images come to your minds when you speak those words each Lord's Day? What does it mean for us as the Body of Christ to say, "We believe in the Holy Ghost"?

The word "believe" in the Apostles' Creed means "to trust," thus when we profess our faith in "the Holy Ghost," or in "the Holy Spirit," we are literally saying, "I trust the Holy Spirit," and that is precisely what the young boy was asking his mother: "Can I trust this Holy Ghost? Is He friendly?" Yet one must take an additional step and ask, "Who is this Holy Ghost whom we profess to trust?" As we consider our Old and New Testament lessons for this Lord's Day, perhaps we can discover some answers to this Lenten quest.

Who is this Holy Ghost? Who is the Holy Spirit? The Holy Spirit is none other than God himself! In the Old Testament, the Hebrew word for "spirit" is *ruach*. According to the content, the word *ruach* can be translated as "wind," "storm," or "breeze." However, more often, the word ruach points to the movement of air caused by the breath. So in the Old Testament, we see that the "holy ruach" or the "Holy Spirit" is literally the breath of God the Creator. It is the very essence of God—that which gives life to the creation.

In his book, *The Doctrine of the Holy Spirit*, Hendrikus Berkhof has written these words, "Spirit means that God is a vital God, who grants vitality to His creation. Therefore I would propose this definition of the Spirit: It is God's inspiring breath by which he grants life in creation."

Our God is a living, acting, breathing God, and He gives life to humanity by putting his own *ruach*, his very life and being, his own Spirit within them. In the older of the two creation accounts, the writer describes the creation of humanity in this manner "God breathed into his nostrils the breath of life; and man became a living being" (Gen. 2:7). God gave life to humanity by blowing his spirit, his life, his breath into us.

As long as God's breath, God's *ruach*, God's spirit is in men and women, they live. In the 104th Psalm, the writer mentions the importance of having God's breath within one's self: "When thou takest away their breath (literally their breath), they die and return to their dust." Thus life for human beings is dependent upon having the Spirit of God, the breath of God within us; that is why the psalmist cries out in our lesson from the Psalter for today: "Cast me not away from thy presence, and take not thy holy spirit from me." If the holy breath of God is missing, one does not have life.

We South Carolinians grew up with this motto *Dum Spiro Spero*, which means, "While I breathe, I hope." I do not know if the founding fathers and mothers realized how theological their statement is. Since they were South Carolinians they must have known. *Dum Spiro Spero*. While I have God's breath, I have hope because I have life.

Now how does one manage to keep God's *ruach*, God's breath, God's spirit within him/her, and thus avoid death? Through obedience. In the second chapter of Genesis, we hear the Lord speaking to Adam, "You may freely eat of every tree of the garden but of the tree of the knowledge of good and evil you shall not eat, for in the day that you eat of it you shall die." In other words, disobedience results in the loss of God's life giving breath.

We all know the story of Adam and Eve. The man and woman disobeyed God's command by eating the forbidden fruit. Their disobedience resulted in a broken relationship with God, who expelled them from paradise. The first parents did not live forever because God, through his judgment of their disobedience, removed his holy breath from them.

Yet the Creator God is also the Redeemer God. He, whose nature it is to share his life, his breath, his spirit with each human being whom he has fashioned and whom he loves, was unwilling to let his fallen creations go to hell. He gave his disobedient creatures another chance to have the Creator's life giving breath within them forever.

Wolfhart Pannenberg writes these words in his book, *The Apostles' Creed:* "In the Old Testament, we see that the Spirit of God is understood as the origin and power of life. In the New Testament, the Spirit is understood as the origin and power of new life." As I said in the past, our Lenten quest is understood in light of the cross. Thus we must always seek to understand the Holy spirit in the light of the cross of Jesus Christ.

In his book, *An Introduction to the Theology of the New Testament*, Alan Richardson writes. "God's Spirit is God acting in Jesus Christ." God's Spirit, i.e., God himself with his life giving breath by giving up his own breath. The Son of God died in our place. He took upon himself the judgment of our disobedience. Jesus received our death sentence as John says, by bowing his head on the cross and giving up his spirit by giving up the life giving breath of God.

Why does the Spirit of God act in Jesus Christ? Why does the Son of God give up his breath in death? Jesus breathes his last in order that you and I might breathe forever, in order that God might bring us out of our state of death and disobedience. Throughout the Gospel of John, "Life," is the message of hope offered to those who believe. John records these words of Jesus. "I came that you may have life, and have it abundantly." You and I breathe because Jesus gave up his breath on the cross. You and I live because Jesus died in our place on the cross. The Spirit of God is God in action on the cross. Through the death of the Son, the Father destroys our disobedience.

Yet, one must also say that the Spirit of God is God in action through the resurrection of Jesus. By breathing his breath of life into the corpse of our Savior, God raised Jesus from the dead, and thus destroyed sin and death once and for all for those who believe in the Son of God.

Thus the new breath of God, eternal life, is given to the disciples on Easter evening. John tells us in his Gospel that the risen Christ appeared to the disciples who were hiding behind barred doors. Jesus spoke to them and said, "Peace be with you. As the Father has sent me, even so I send you." John goes on to tell us that when Jesus had spoken these words, he breathed on them, and said to them, "Receive the Holy Spirit."

What does it mean that the Risen Lord breathed on the disciples and said, "Receive the Holy spirit"? Let us refer to Alan Richardson's book once again where he writes, "God's Spirit is God acting."

After the resurrection God works and acts in a new way in us. My former theology professor, Shirley Guthrie, says that God has three ways of being God: (1) As God the Father over us. (2) As God the Son with us. (3) As God the Holy Spirit in us. Who is this Holy spirit? God's Holy spirit is God acting, working, and living in us. Thus the risen Christ breathed on the disciples, and God's holy breath, God's holy spirit, God's holy presence came into them. In our text for today, we see this reality in the words of Jesus: "In that day you will know that I am in my Father, and you in me, and I in you." Who is the Holy Spirit? The Holy Spirit is none other than God himself who destroyed sin and death in the cross and resurrection of Jesus Christ, and who grants to us his holy breath, eternal life, by living in us. The Holy Spirit is God in us.

The question that we must ask this morning is what difference does it make in your life and in mine that God lives in you and me through his Holy Spirit?

In our New Testament lesson of today, John records these words of Jesus: "If you love me, you will keep my commandments. And I will pray the Father, and he will give you another helper to be with you forever."

Now John is not implying, through these words of our Lord, that God's love and acceptance of us is dependent upon our obedience as it was in the Garden of Eden. God has already accepted us in the death and resurrection of our Savior. Even though we disobey, God does not take his holy breath from us, as he took it from Adam, because Jesus gave up his breath in our behalf.

Yet obedience and love are conditions that rule our new life. John says that when the helper comes, when the Holy Spirit comes, he will work in the lives of believers in such a way that they will become like Jesus Christ, the new Adam, the new humanity, by keeping the commandments of Jesus. What difference his presence in our lives makes is that he makes us more like the Savior each day, by helping us to keep the commandments of Jesus.

The first commandment of Jesus is "You shall love the Lord your God with all your heart, and with all your soul, and with all your mind." The Holy Spirit enables us to love God and to trust God as our Father. It is the Spirit's work which helps us to trust God for our salvation while forgetting our sinful past. It is the Spirit's work which teaches us to trust God in daily living even though danger constantly lurks in our neighborhoods and death looms on the horizon as nations threaten to rise up against one another.

The Spirit teaches us to cry "Abba, Father," and as we make such a cry, we come to trust him, knowing that "neither death, nor life, nor principalities, nor powers will be able to separate us from the love of God in Christ Jesus our Lord." The Holy Spirit helps us to love and trust God in such a way that we can always pray with the Savior, "Thy will be done."

The second commandment of Jesus is this: "A new commandment I give to you, that you love one another even as I have loved you." Where the Spirit is at work in our lives, we learn to love one another. There can be no jealousy, no harsh feelings toward others, no grudges, no unwillingness to forgive because the Holy Spirit makes a difference in our lives. He teaches us to love and forgive one another even as we have been loved and forgiven by Jesus Christ.

The final commandment of the Lord is that "When the Holy Spirit has come upon you, you shall be my witnesses in Jerusalem, and in all Judea and Samaria, and to the end of the earth." In his book, *The Humility of God*, John Macquarrie writes, "Thus to say that God is Spirit is to say that it belongs to his very nature to pour himself out. He has continued to go forth from himself throughout the history of the creation."

The Holy Spirit will not allow us to live for ourselves. He will not allow us to live a private life. Rather He teaches us to pour ourselves out, to give ourselves away in servanthood, to live for others after the manner of our Savior. Where there is an unwillingness to serve, the Holy Spirit is not present. God's Spirit works in us to make us like the Savior by walking in His steps of service.

Who is the Holy Spirit? He is God in us. What difference does the Spirit make by living in us? He teaches us each day how to live like the Savior. In the words of the young boy, "Is he friendly?" He is more than friendly. He is the loving God whose breath we have because His Son has given his breath up for us.

Prayer

Come Holy Spirit and teach us what it means to trust, to love, and to serve after the manner of our Savior even Jesus Christ. Amen.

The Cup of Christ
Old Testament: Psalm 34
New Testament : Matthew 26: 36-46

When we are young and inexperienced, most of us will try anything at least once. When the First Presbyterian Church at Rock Hill extended a call to me in 1974, I immediately embraced the challenge. Some of my friends and colleagues in Charleston urged me to approach that opportunity with caution. Older and wiser, those ministers knew the struggles and pain of "putting Humpty-Dumpty back together again."

That magnificent, old church had experienced a traumatic split in 1973, and most of the people to whom I turned for advice felt that the people of Rock Hill deserved someone with a few grey hairs and a skin as tough as elephant hide. At that time, I was twenty-seven: I had no grey hairs and my skin was very thin. I am glad that I did not listen to the good advice that some of my friends sought to give me. I would not take anything for those five years that I lived and worked with the great people of Rock Hill.

However, there were many times during the first year of my ministry in Rock Hill that I wished I had listened to those caring Charlestonian voices who had urged me to approach the challenge with caution. "Why didn't I listen to them? Why did I ever come here?" I asked myself many times. The church was almost destroyed by that satanic split, and during those first few months I was afraid that the church would fold—and so would I.

I shall never forget standing in our bedroom closet one Sunday after worship services, weeping uncontrollably. I turned to Judy, who was a constant source of encouragement, and said, "I hope that in five years I can say, 'God, it was worth it.'" It was and I did!

On a cold December morning, the first December that we lived in Rock Hill, I got into my car and started driving, not knowing where I was going. The emotional pressures were more than I could take. I wanted to lose myself somewhere. I finally drove to the presbytery's camp where I walked through the woods for what seemed like an eternity. During the summer those woods were always alive with plants, animals, mosquitoes, and the laughter of children. The only sign of life on that particular day of wandering and searching were the bare oak trees that slowly swayed with the wind. Their "bareness" reminded me of the condition of my soul, and only the "crunching" sound of the leaves under my feet assured me that I was alive. I walked. I ran. I cried. I screamed. I felt like a total failure.

Suddenly I found myself tumbling down an embankment. It must have been an amusing sight—arms and legs going in all different directions. It was not amusing to me. At the bottom of the hill I lay flat on my back, and to my disappointment I was alive and unhurt. For a long time I did not move because it felt good to lie in a bed of leaves. The rays of the sun warmed my "icy" face.

To my surprise, I discovered life. Perched in a gum tree above me, a bird sang. Its song soothed my sorrow. After a few moments, my "feathered" friend began to descend. Limb by limb, it came closer to me until it was only a few feet above my head. I lay motionlessly, hoping that it would come even closer. When it saw that I was O.K., it flew away. Immediately I thought of Elijah and Francis of Assisi. In that moment, I believed, and I still believe that God had ministered to me through one of His smallest creatures.

I walked out of the woods on that December day a new person. The bird had given me strength and hope. I still had many difficult days in Rock Hill, but never again did I doubt that the church or I would make it.

All of us need a private place where we can bare our souls to God. Jesus had such a place in the Garden of Gethsemane. Gethsemane means "olive press," and probably it was an olive grove on the Mount of Olives where Jesus went many times with His disciples to pray and sleep. It was so familiar that Judas knew where to lead the men who arrested Jesus.

Matthew's account of our Lord's agony in Gethsemane is told in stark simplicity and perhaps it is as moving as anything that one can find in all of literature. As they entered Gethsemane, Matthew tells us that Jesus left eight of the disciples on the fringe of the grove. He then took with Him Peter and the sons of Zebedee, James and John, to witness His vigil and spiritual struggle. These three disciples had shared His glory on the Mount of Transfiguration, and in Gethsemane they were asked to share the Savior's pain.

Our Lord knew that all three would need to be strengthened by witnessing His struggle. After the meal in the upper room Jesus said to them, "You will fall away from me this night; for it is written, 'I will strike the shepherd, and the sheep of the flock will be scattered.' But after I am raised up, I will go before you to Galilee." Impetuous Peter spoke up, "Though they all fall away because of you, I will never fall away."

Jesus responded to Peter's pledge, "Truly I say to you, this very night, before the cock crows, you will deny me three times." The "cock crow" was the trumpet note that sounded the third Roman watch between midnight and three o'clock. Peter needed to watch and pray with Jesus in order that his willing spirit would not be mastered by the weakness and fear of the flesh during those wee hours of the morning.

James and John had asked on one occasion to sit on either side of Jesus in the kingdom of heaven. Jesus responded to their request by asking, "Are you able to drink the cup I drink or to be baptized with the baptism with which I am baptized?" In other words, "Are you able to die with me and for me?" The sons of thunder retorted, "We are able." Jesus responded, "The cup that I drink you will drink."

Our Lord knew that James and John would be martyred in years to come, and they could obtain strength to face their hour by sharing Jesus' hour.

In describing our Lord's agony, Matthew has borrowed heavily from Mark. Both accounts are brimming with symbolism. The three times that Jesus prayed and three times that He returned to find the sleeping disciples are matched with Peter's denials, with the three hours of agony on the cross, and with the three days our Lord spent in the tomb.

To those three disciples, who would someday share the same destiny as our Lord, Jesus said, "My soul is very sorrowful, even to death." A deadly desolation had descended upon the Christ, and He shared His agony with the disciples in words that are reminiscent of Psalm 43: "Why are you cast down, O my soul, and why are you disquieted within me?" In other words, "I am sunk in misery. My sorrow is killing me. Remain here and watch with me."

Moving a little farther away, Luke tells us about a stone's throw, Jesus fell on His face and prayed, "My father, if it be possible, let this cup pass from me; nevertheless, not as I will, but as Thou wilt." Do the words that Jesus spoke to the disciples, "My soul is very sorrowful, even to death," and the words He spoke to God, "Father let this cup pass from me," imply that our Lord was afraid of dying? Could the One who came from God, who said, "In my Father's house are many mansions," who spoke calmly to His disciples in Galilee about His death and resurrection, and who maintained an attitude of calm serenity during His arrest, trial and execution, fear death? By no means.

Then why did Jesus go to Gethsemane? Why did He express His sorrow? Why did He need the presence of friends to strengthen Him? Why did He pray, "Father, if it be possible, let this cup pass from me?" And wasn't the cup that He feared, the cup of death?

Jesus did not fear death. He is the Lord of resurrection! The dreadful sorrow and anxiety out of which the prayer for the passing of the cup came was not an expression of fear of physical suffering. Rather it was the horror of the Son who had to experience alienation from the Father because the Son then assumed the world's judgment. It was the horror of the cross: *Eli, Eli, lama sabach-tha-ni?* That is, "My God, my God, why hast Thou forsaken me?"

On the cross, Jesus accepted the guilt of humankind upon Himself. He took the sinner's place, your place and mine, and experienced the punishment that our sins deserve. He gave His life as a ransom for many.

In the Old Testament, the cup was a metaphor that was used for punishment and retribution. Isaiah spoke of the cup in this manner, "Rouse yourself, O Jerusalem, you who have drunk at the hand of the Lord the cup of His wrath, who have drunk to the dregs the bowl of staggering." In the past, the sinner had to drink the cup of God's wrath and punishment. No longer is that true for those who are in Christ Jesus. On the cross, our Lord drank the cup of wrath for us. Drinking that cup brought anguish to Jesus. Bearing our guilt and punishment meant enduring His Father's displeasure over our sin. Accepting our judgment meant suffering the depth of Hell where one is alienated from the love of the Father, and is the meaning of the cry from the Cross, "My God, my God, why have You forsaken me?" The Christ entered the gates of hell for you and me.

Our Lord was not afraid to die. He did not fear whips, thorns, nails, spears and angry mobs. He was not afraid of crucifixion, but He was afraid. He feared the pain of separation and alienation from the Father—the cost He must pay for accepting our judgment. Jesus prayed three times, "My Father, if it be possible, let this cup pass from me; nevertheless, not what I will but what Thou wilt." In other words, "If there is any other way to redeem Your world without my having to experience separation from You, then let it be so." Yet He qualified His prayer by saying, "If that is not possible, then let Your will be done."

Luke informs us that Jesus' agony over His impending separation from God was so great that His sweat became like great drops of blood falling down upon the ground: "My Father, if it be possible, let this cup pass from me." Although the disciples allow their master to struggle alone, God does not. A favorite hymn of mine that we often sing during Lent is "Tis Midnight; and On Olive's Brow." The third verse rings forth with power and assurance:

> Tis midnight; and for others guilt,
> The Man of sorrow weeps in blood;
> Yet He that hath in anguish knelt
> Is not forsaken by His God.

Although the Savior would experience the alienation from God on the cross, the judgment for our sin, God would not let Him pray alone in Gethsemane. Luke's gospel informs us that an angel from heaven appeared to strengthen Him in those agonizing moments. Perhaps the angel assured the Christ that there was no other way to save the world. He had been sent as the Savior, and He must drink the bitter cup in our behalf.

Perhaps the angel reminded Jesus of the heavenly voice that was heard at His baptism in the Jordan: "This is my beloved Son in whom I am well pleased." In the moment of agony when it would have been easy to flee to the other side of the Mt. of Olives to Bethany and then on to the safe confines of Galilee, Jesus was strengthened to face and accept the will of His Father, even if it meant suffering alienation from Him.

As approaching voices interrupted the silence of the garden and flickering torches drove away the heavy darkness, Jesus turned from His praying and said to His disciples, "Are you still sleeping and taking your rest? Behold the hour is at hand, and the Son of man is betrayed into the hands of sinners. Rise, let us be going."

That last sentence, "Rise, let us be going," is the climax of the vigil in Gethsemane. It is the most powerful sentence in the entire account. Matthew never allows his readers to think that Jesus was a helpless victim of circumstance. As the Christ, He is always the master of the hour. His time is at hand, the time in which He must drink the inescapable cup. So He says to those who sleep, "Rise, let us be going." The Savior, having conquered His moment of agony, goes forth to do the will of His Father and to obtain our salvation. I find strength and encouragement in that statement: "Rise, let us be going."

James Martineau has written these words:

> A voice from the midnight air
> Where Kedron's moonlit waters stray,
> Weeps forth, in agony of prayer,
> O Father, take this cup away!
>
> Ah, Thou, who sorrows unto death,
> We conquer in Thy mortal fray;
> And earth for all her children saith,
> O God, take not this cup away.

Let us conclude this morning by returning to the introduction of the sermon. Those of us who walk through the woods or in the loneliness of our home or apartment, searching for strength in which to face our difficult hours, will find strength in the suffering Savior who agonized alone in Gethsemane. The One who said, "Rise, let us be going," has drunk the cup in our behalf. He has obtained the victory for us, and nothing—not even the gates of hell—shall prevail against us.

Several years ago I was called to the bedside of a stranger who was slowly dying. I held her frail hand and said very little. What does one say in such painful moments? When the time came for me to leave, I asked this lady if she would like for me to pray for her. When she whispered, "Yes," I asked, "What would you like for me to pray?" Immediately she responded, "Pray that I shall remain faithful in the midst of my suffering." Here is one who understood the meaning of the words, "Rise, let us be going."

May those of us who must face the struggle and uncertainty of the coming hours turn to the words of the triumphant Savior: "Rise, let us be going." Let us face the future with the certainty that we are loved because Christ has drunk the cup for us. Such knowledge enables us to say, "If God is for us who can be against us? He who did not spare His own Son but gave Him up for us all, will He not also give us all things with Him? In all these things we are more than conquerors through Him." "Rise, let us be going!" Let us meet our future with confidence for Christ has obtained victory for us.

Prayer

At times, Our Father, the struggle is more than we can bear. May our Lord's struggle in Gethsemane remind us that He has obtained victory for us all. Therefore, O Lord, help us to rise and to face the future with the certainty that nothing can separate us from the love of God in Christ Jesus our Lord. Amen

Easter That Comes Before Lent

Psalm 23

Matthew 20: 1-20

The last words spoken from the cross on Good Friday are the haunting but triumphant words of the dying Savior, "It is finished." Then there is the silence of darkness and the reality of death. It is finished. The Savior's earthly life and ministry have come to a completion. The saving blood of the cross covers our sin. "Earth's redeeming work is done." It is finished.

However, something significant goes unnoticed in that impressive moment. Jesus is dead; his lips are sealed shut by the absence of breath. But then God speaks in a language of His own. As Matthew says about that gory but glorious event at Golgotha:

"And behold, the curtain of the Temple was torn in two from top to bottom and the earth shook, and the rocks were split."

When Jesus died, the earth quaked. God always has the last word about suffering and death. After the singular silence of Saturday comes the glorious announcement of resurrection. In rare form Matthew writes these words:

> Now after the sabbath, toward the dawn
> of the first day of the week, Mary Magdalene
> and the other Mary went to see the sepulchre.
> And behold there was a great earth quake
> For an angel of the lord descended
> from heaven and rolled back the stone, and sat
> upon it. His appearance was like lightning, and
> his raiment white as snow. And for fear of him
> the guards trembled and became like dead men.

On Easter morning the earth quaked and the guards trembled, because God always has the last word about death and His final word is seen and felt in the shaking of the earth and in the quaking fear of the guards.

In both the Old and New Testament the earthquake denotes the presence and the interventions of God among the people of earth and it reveals His greatness as the God of the Covenant.

The Easter Event of the Old Testament, as it were, is the Passover and the Crossing of the Red Sea. By day the Savior God led the erstwhile slaves with the pillar of cloud, and by night with the pillar of fire 'til He brought them safely to the holy mount of Sinai. There He spoke to them words of Resurrection. Listen to how the psalmist (68:8) described that epiphany: "The earth shook, the heavens dropped at the presence of God; even Sinai itself was moved at the coming of God."

And the earth moved. It trembled. It quaked. It shook. It always does when God visits earth with His power to destroy death's dominion, thereby freeing his people from the shackles of non-being.

No matter how strong one's faith is, it always seems that death has the last word over earth's children. To appreciate the beauty of the Easter gospel, one must take careful note of the last sentence in the preceding chapter. The last word from Good Friday is from the procurator of Judea who passed and pronounced the death sentence of the Savior; Pilate said to them, "You have a guard of soldiers; Go make the tomb as secure as you can. And they went and made the sepulcher secure by sealing the stone and setting a guard."

The earth shook on Good Friday, but no one would heed its trembling. In their pain and sorrow the disciples cowered in hiding, save one, Joseph of Arimathaea, who took the limp body of our Lord from the cross, wrapped it in a linen shroud and lay it in his own new tomb. Then he rolled a great stone to the door of the grave and as Matthew says, he then departed.

Mary Magdalene and the other Mary were there, sitting opposite the sepulcher. They were the only ones other than Joseph of Arimathea who knew the whereabouts of Jesus' tomb. And their hearts were heavy with sorrow.

As Dostoevski writes, "The people surrounding the dead man experienced the most terrible consternation which had crushed their hopes and their convictions."

Death has a way of doing that to every human in the face of sorrow even though the earth shakes.

On Good Friday the earth trembled, but the authorities responsible for our Lord's crucifixion did not notice because they believed that death always had the last word. So they secured the sepulcher by sealing the stone while setting a guard. But wait a minute. If death has the final word, why secure the grave? Why set a guard who will turn away would be grave robbers?

Through the long watch of the night, the guards waited as they were commanded—and the disciples slept—or something! Then Matthew reveals a thought too great for human fears to comprehend: "Now after the Sabbath toward the dawn of the first day of the week, Mary Magdalene and the other Mary went to see the sepulcher. And behold there was a great earthquake for an angel of the Lord descended from heaven and came and rolled back the stone and sat upon it. His appearance was like lightning, and his raiment white as snow. And for fear of him the guards trembled and became like dead men." When the earth shakes so do unbelievers and some believers. Heaven visits earth symbolized by the earthquake. Heaven defeats the dominion of earthly death, symbolized by the angel sitting on the stone. And earth trembles in fear symbolized by the guards' immobilization.

But the angel said to the women, "Do not be afraid." How can one not fear when humans stand before that which is holy? Yet the angelic words are comforting. "Do not be afraid; for I know that you seek Jesus who was crucified. He is not here; for He is risen, as he said."

Death and those who would inflict its savage presence upon us does not have the final word. God does. He always does—and the earth shakes.

In her poem titled "Substitution", Elizabeth Barrett Browning wrote these words:

> When some beloved voice that was to you
> Both sound and sweetness, faileth suddenly,
> And silence against which you dare not cry,
> Aches round you like a strong disease and new,
> What hope? What help? What music will undo
> that silence to your sense?
> Speak Thou, availing Christ and fill this pause.

And the earth shook. God filled this pause between the pain of separation and the reunion of resurrection by shaking His earth, His way of saying that His Son lives in spite of the worst that humanity can do. The Risen Christ always has the last word, and His final word is this: "Because I live, you shall live also." And the earth shook.

What meaning do these words, "And the earth shook" have for you and me during this holy Eastertide? If I may be so personal, let me tell you what the shaking earth means to me.

Each of us has stood over a grave of someone we love dearly.

You have. I have. We all have. It hurts deeply like no other human pain. And one of the most difficult tasks I have to do as a minister is to officiate funerals of people I love and of people you love. To see the hurt and tears of people I care about is heart-rending. But in each and every case, if we put our feet on the ground, we can feel the earth shake as God's voice resounds through the dark, uncertain moment, assuring us that the one we love is not dead, but resides in the safe haven of heaven.

Christine Fodera of Louisville wrote recently in *Readers Digest* about an amazing experience she and her husband had. Their priest had asked her husband Sam to do some rewiring in the confessionals. The only way to reach the wiring was to enter the attic above the altar and crawl over the ceiling by balancing on the rafters. Concerned for her husband's safety, Christine waited in a pew.

Unbeknownst to Christine, some other people were congregating in the vestibule. They paid little attention to her, assuming that she was praying.

Worried about her husband, she looked up toward the ceiling and yelled, "Sam, Sam are you up there? Did you make it okay?"

There was quite an outburst from the Vestibule when Sam's hearty voice echoed down, "Yes, I made it up here just fine." And the earth shook.

You see, that is what the Easter faith means for all of us who find ourselves sitting in a cemetery around the grave of a loved one and the earth suddenly starts shaking under our feet. God is having the last word and He dries our tears within his trembling earth saying to our shivering souls, "Your loved one has made it up here just fine."

Every Sunday morning we say these words, "I believe in the communion of the saints, the forgiveness of sin, the resurrection of the body, and the life everlasting."

These words of the Apostles Creed are for us either an empty ritual of rote or we believe them with such vigor that the earth literally shakes beneath our feet.

The earth shook in the cemetery as God speaks to his grieving children,

> In my Father's house are many mansions.
> If it were not so I would have told you.
> And if I go and prepare a place for you, I
> will come again and take you unto myself,
> that where I am, you may be also.

"Yes, I made it up here just fine," is the victorious message of the saints above, and it is the certain hope of every saint on earth . . . your hope, my hope, our hope.

You seek Jesus who was crucified. He is not here; for He has risen, as He said and "the earth shook".

Secondly, the Easter message, proclaimed in the shaking of the earth, states that God not only has the final word over death, but He also has the final word over life.

Since Christ lives, life with all of its difficult struggles has meaning and purpose moving toward closure, yet not until God's purpose for our living on this earth is fulfilled.

There are times that you and I may feel that we are literally hanging on to the very end of our rope. Suddenly the earth shakes, and we realize there is one more knot to which we can cling; it is the knot of grace, the reality of resurrection, the certainty that the risen Christ destroys the death-like experiences which we encounter in living when at time, dying seems easier than living.

However, no believer in the risen Christ can conceive of the possibility of futility because the risen Christ lives within us, transforming this life of discouragement into hope and meaning.

Consider what the resurrection did for Peter's life. His was a life that went from hiding in the shadows of denial to a life that so forcibly proclaimed the resurrection of Christ that his very shadow which fell over the sick and dying brought instant healing and restoration

Our shadows can and do have that same effect and impact no matter how low life stoops. The reality is this: Christ is risen from the grave, and His resurrection restores meaning to life, no matter what our station.

Christ's resurrection gives us eternal life. In the Gospels, eternal life is not only quantitative it is also qualitative. That is why the Savior said, "I came that you may have life, and have it abundantly". Or as the Apostle wrote, "I can do all things through Christ who strengthens me."

Easter means that you and I can face every experience in life with the power of resurrection—the power of the one who speaks in such a manner that the earth shakes beneath our feet.

If you and I feel dead on the inside, then let us open our hearts to his promise: Because I live, you shall live also now and forevermore.

"Now after the Sabbath, toward the dawn of the first day of the week, Mary Magdalene and the other Mary went to see the sepulcher . . . An angel of the Lord descended from heaven and rolled back the stone."

The angel said unto the women, "Do not be afraid. For I know that you seek Jesus who was crucified. He is not here; for He is risen as he said."

And the earth shook. And you know something? It still does.

Prayer

O blessed God who has destroyed death's domain, grant us
grace to believe and to sing these words: "The kingdom of
the world has become the kingdom of our Lord and of His Christ;
and He shall reign forever and ever.

The Resurrected

Jeremiah 1: 1-10

Mark 2: 13-17

I am about to make a statement that few preachers want to make. It is a dangerous comment for anyone who stands to preach behind a pulpit. I want you to close your eyes for a few seconds.

Do not get too comfortable and please do not go to sleep. But close your eyes. Now concentrate on a face. It is not just any face; rather it is the face of God—a face that not even Moses was allowed to see. The face of God is none other than the face of Jesus Christ.

What is it that you see on the back of your eye lids? Do you notice his olive complexion which is enhanced by a dark, distinct beard? However, if we look closely we notice that his pleasant face is drawn with pain. Blood is caked on his forehead where the razor sharp thorns of his man-made crown pierces his hair line. Perspiration pours down his cheeks under the oppressive heat of the noonday sun. Flies and gnats buzz aggravatingly around his swollen ears and misty eyes.

His arms are stretched above his head with his wrists tied to a splintery crossbeam, and his hands are nailed fast with bone-crushing spikes! Gravity pulls his body downward—a pull so heavy that the only way the Savior can breathe is to push himself upward with his nail-torn feet, and with each push, the flesh of his feet tears even more.

The face imprinted on your eye lids is the face of agonizing love. It is the face of God himself, revealed in the face of the dying Son of God.

Now look closely and listen carefully in the silence of your soul. Watch his lips move and listen thankfully as he utters your name. Hear distinctly what he says to you and me. Do you hear his voice, the voice of the victorious Lord? He calls to you and says, I am suffering for you. I am dying for you. I will be raised for you. I will ascend to my Father's right hand where I will reign for you. My dying love covers your sins with my flowing blood, and your past mistakes and failures are gone and forgotten.

My resurrection love takes away the fear and dread of death and the death of dying is now accomplished. When you breathe your last breath, I shall greet you with open arms and lead you into my heavenly kingdom.

My ascending love only enhances your life. Even though my

body is not physically present, you see me in the life of the Church which is now my earthly body. But I live and dwell in you every minute of the day strengthening and guiding you in all that you do and say.

Now, follow me. Follow me. Serve me, for I have a purpose and plan for your life.

Open your eyes.

What do you and I do with that face? What do we do with the words of the Savior—personal words to each of us. Words which call us to follow and serve him.

A call to serve God is always a compelling call. For how does one not answer the call from the Christ who has died in our place?

Consider God's call to Jeremiah in today's text. Baruch, Jeremiah's scribe, tells us that God called a young boy, son of the priest Hilkiah from Anathoth a small village three miles north of Jerusalem, to perform an adult task. A young boy was to serve as a prophet, a preacher during a very difficult and decisive time in Judah's history.

Baruch is careful to tell us that God's call to Jeremiah came during the thirteenth year of Josiah's reign. He goes on to say that it also came during the reign of Jehorakim and Zedekiah.

Baruch's choice of identifying kings with whom Jeremiah worked reminds me of a story that used to float around seminary when I was a student.

A former football player from the University of Georgia entered Columbia Seminary years ago. He was a good ole Georgia boy but his academic skills were lacking. As the fall term came to a close, this former football player worried about his final exam in his Old Testament course.

One of his classmates sought to allay his anxiety by saying, "Don't worry, the professor has given the same final exam for the last ten years. All you have to do is memorize all the Kings of Israel and Judah and the dates of their reigns, and you will get an A."

On exam day, all the students walked into the classroom fully prepared to name all the Kings of Israel and Judah. However, the professor for the first time in a decade changed his exam. He gave the students this essay question, "Distinguish between the major and minor prophets and tell why."

All the students drew a blank except the erstwhile football player from Georgia who wrote and wrote and wrote. When the professor returned the exams, everyone received an "F" except the "Georgia boy" who received an "A".

Confused by the young man's good grade, several of the students asked to see his test paper. To their surprise, the students who had failed found these words written on the football player's paper: "Who am I, a sinner in God's eyes, to decide which prophet made a major contribution and which prophet made a minor contribution in the service of God's kingdom, but as for the Kings of Israel and Judah, they are as follows. . ."

Like the former football player from Georgia, Jeremiah was well acquainted with the Kings of Judah. Some listened to him, but most laughed at his youthful words. God called Jeremiah in the 13th year of Josiah's reign, 620 years before the birth of Christ. It is this call, this compelling call that I want us to consider briefly.

Jeremiah says, "Now the word of the Lord came to me saying before I formed you in the womb I knew you, and before you were born I consecrated you. I appointed you as a prophet to the nations."

Isaiah makes a similar claim when he says, "The Lord called me from the womb." The Apostle Paul in his letter to the Galatians writes, "But when he had set me apart before I was born, and had called me through his grace, I did not confer with the flesh and blood but I went away into Arabia."

As with the servants of old, so it is with every believer in Christ. God has a divine plan for each of us, which is prior, not only to our response, but also to our birth. To the Ephesians, Paul wrote, "God chose us in Christ before the foundation of the world."

A young child once asked of her mother, "Where was I before I was born?" To which her mother replied, "In the mind of God." Before time existed, you and I were in the mind of God.

One notices in Jeremiah's call four active verbs: I formed you. I knew you. I consecrated you. I appointed you. Each verb enhances our call from God.

The verb "formed" is used in this text as it is read in the Genesis account of creation ". . . then the Lord God formed Adam from dust, and breathed into his nostrils the breath of life." When Jeremiah tells of his experience of watching the potter at his wheel, we see that God's creative activity is like that of a potter, who takes us from his mind and shapes and forms us for a specific purpose. The hand of God has formed each one of us as distinct and unique creatures for one purpose: To serve Him.

The verb "knew" in this Hebrew context means to have regard for a chosen object. In other words, God is saying to Jeremiah and to us, "Before I formed you, I knew you," that is "I loved you." God has proved his love for us in the face we observed a few minutes ago and it is that love, you see, that compels us to answer his call.

The verb "consecrated" might better be expressed with the word separated, i.e., "Before you were born, I separated you, I set you apart, like vessels of the Temple, for a holy use, for my use. Thus we discover our purpose in life is to live as a vessel of God.

The verb "appointed" in the text really means given. "Before you were born, I gave you to the world as a gift to my people where you make a difference in their lives."

However, notice what happens when we humans hear these four verbs spoken to us in God's call. Jeremiah responded by saying, "Ah, Lord God. Behold, I do not know how to speak, for I am only a youth."

Many of the biblical characters found excuses for not serving God. Moses balked at the voice which came from the burning bush: "Lord, I am not eloquent enough to speak for you." Yet Moses was eloquent with excuses. Isaiah and Gideon made the excuses that they were unworthy. Jonah simply ran away.

Who can forget the excuse of St. Augustine, the great 5th century theologian who prayed, "Grant me chastity and continence, O Lord, but not yet." In other words, I want to serve you, God, but I want to have some fun in life first.

When God called Jeremiah to do a task, he protested, saying, "No. I am too young. I am inexperienced. Find someone else."

How eloquent you and I have become with our excuses. Through the centuries, God has heard them all. I suppose the most favorite excuse that we use today is "I'm just too busy." Have you ever used it? It's my favorite. Yet God wants and needs busy people. They are the ones who can get the job done.

Why do we flippantly fling our excuses into the face of God, that face which reveals dying love? We do so because serving God is never easy. As the writer of Hebrews says, "It is a fearful thing to fall into the hands of the living God."

Serving Christ means the cross. Serving the living Lord means death. Answering the call of God means dying to self and living to God. One finds it easier to make an excuse than to die. It is easier to come up with some excuse than to put oneself at the disposal of Christ.

Yet one must remember that in the midst of his/her attempts to find adequate excuses, God's call is always a compelling call. The one who sought no excuse to keep from dying in our place on the cross will never accept our excuses. The church may, but not her Lord. He is persistent in His grace. "Do not say, 'I am only a youth' for to all whom I send you, you shall go, and whatever I command you, you shall speak. Be not afraid, for I am with you."

In his book, *The Courage To Be*, Paul Tillich writes,

> Human beings desire to escape God . . . persons of all
> kinds, prophets and reformers, saints and atheists, believ-
> ers and unbelievers have the same experience. It is safe to
> say that a person who has never tried to flee God has never
> experienced the God who is really God.

The name Jeremiah means, "Yahweh exalts." The very name of
the prophet attests to the fact that God never sends us out in our own
strength, but in the strength of God. The very essence of knowing
God is to know his delivering strength and power. As the Apostle Paul
believed, "I can do all things in Christ who strengthens me." Do we
hear those words, "I can do anything, anything because it is God who
calls and God always gives the wherewith to do it."

In the season that lies ahead, the season of discipleship and the
season of stewardship. God's call will come to each of us. Before we
seek to make excuses and before we say no, let us close our eyes and
see the face of dying love.

How will we answer? Do we have any choice but to say with the
Apostle, "Necessity is laid upon me"?

Early Easter Events

The Gospels maintain a sense of urgency in their use of the word early. Mark writes "After the Sabbath was over, Mary Magdalene, and Mary, the mother of James and Salome, brought spices to go and anoint the body of Jesus. Very early on Sunday morning at sunrise, they went to the tomb."

Luke proffers this statement. "Very early on Sunday morning, the women went to the tomb carrying spices they had prepared." John follows suit. "Early on Sunday morning while it was still dark, Mary Magdalene went to the tomb."

In our text for this Easter Sunday 2008, Matthew refers to the early hour. "After the Sabbath, as Sunday was dawning." The emphasis on the word *early* reveals that which occurs before the usual or appointed time. Normally the women would be home, still asleep, like the rest of the disciples, for it was very early—still dark. Why were the women on their way so early in the morning?

Jesus died on Friday afternoon shortly before the Sabbath began. Thus, they had to await the passing of the Sabbath during which no work could be done, not even the burial of the dead. So Luke tells us, "Very early on Sunday morning the women went to the tomb carrying spices." Great haste was necessary for in that climate dead bodies decomposed very quickly. So the women came to the tomb very early on Sunday morning while it was still dark to complete burial of their Master and Friend.

"Suddenly," says Matthew, "there was a violent earthquake. An angel of the Lord came down from heaven and rolled the stone away and sat upon it."

On Friday afternoon, when Jesus died, the earth announced the death of the Savior through the quaking of the entire planet. On Sunday morning, the violent earthquake announced the glorious resurrection of our Savior, Jesus Christ.

In the Bible, the earthquake always denoted the presence and the intervention of God among men and women of faith, showing His might and greatness as the God of the Covenant. The Lord made a New Covenant with us through the crucifixion and resurrection of His own dear Son. His death on the cross cleanses us from our sins and His resurrection destroys death's dominion over us—the Covenant of Grace which we accept gratefully through faith.

The earthquake which occurred very early on Sunday morning,

while it was still dark, proclaims to all the earth that God is with us, assuring us that death has no power over us and that eternal life is ours because we believe in the Savior who died late Friday and God raised from the dead very early on Sunday morning.

The jarring of the earth was not caused by Jesus when He departed from the tomb. "When the angels appeared, Jesus had already risen." None of the Gospel writers attempt to describe the resurrection for no human witnessed it. Our Savior left the tomb silently. His dead body was suddenly quickened by the voice of the Father, "My Son, come forth."

Silently, invisibly, wondrously, gloriously the risen Lord passed through the walls of the stone-cold, sealed sepulcher very early on Sunday morning and then the earth quaked, and Gabriel himself came down out of heaven, rolled away the stone and sat upon it, waiting for the arrival of the women who had left home while it was still dark.

This is now a different tomb and it calls for a different watchman, not for keepers of the dead like those of Pilate's guard, but for an angel from the eternal realm—God's own messenger.

I love the way Matthew says it, "And for fear of him the guards did quake and become as dead." The Roman soldiers who guarded the tomb saw the angel from heaven and were struck with terror. They did quake, shaking in fear as the earth shook with joy.

Christ's resurrection is just as terrible for His foes as it is comforting for His friends. The Romans guarded the tomb so that the disciples could not come and steal the body; however, they forgot to guard it against Jesus.

When the women arrived, the angel said unto them, "Do not be afraid. I know you seek Jesus who was crucified. He is not here; He is risen as He said. See the place where the Lord lay."

Why is Jesus not in the grave? Because He is risen from the dead. Here all the blessed news is announced. He whom they left in the sepulcher cold and still on Friday, is not here early on Sunday morning. God raised Him from the dead.

To assure the women further, the angel invites them to come closer to see where the Lord lay. They are to see that not only the tomb is now empty, they are to see the linen wrappings lying undisturbed, as though the body has gone out of them in a miraculous manner, and the head cloth lay by itself.

If Jesus had not been raised from the dead, these women and the disciples would not have had anything to do after the burial was completed early on Sunday morning. Now that Jesus is risen the most blest task awaits these women. The angel speaks as the new day dawns. "Go quickly, now, and tell his disciples that He has been raised from death and now He is going to Galilee ahead of you. There you will see Him. Lo, I did tell you."

The women are not to remain at the tomb in awe. They are not to give in to the fascination of these strange sights. They are not to speculate about all these things they have seen and heard. Rather they are to do something far more important. They are to proclaim the wonderful news of resurrection. This news cannot reach the grieving disciples soon enough, even if it is early, very early in the morning.

These early morning visitors walked to the tomb, filled with sorrow. They ran from the tomb filled with joy entrusted with the proclamation of Jesus' resurrection. The women are called to be the first evangelists, the first preachers of the Word. Their first message is the Lord is Risen!

In his letter to the church in Rome, the Apostle shares these words. "How beautiful are the feet of them that preach the Gospel of Peace and bring glad tidings of good things."

As the women ran to share the angel's news with the disciples, Jesus, the Risen Lord, met them and said to them, "Peace be with you." The women came up to Him, took hold of His feet and worshipped Him. Jesus said, "Fear not." And then our Risen Savior told these faithful servants, "Go and tell my brothers to go to Galilee, and there they will see me."

According to Matthew, this is the first appearance of the risen Lord. The same responsibility of proclaiming the gospel of resurrection the angels had assigned the women to tell, as did Jesus, "tell my brothers."

Grace is given to the disciples that Jesus would call them "brothers." They fled from Him in Gethsemane. Peter had denied Him. All but John hid in fear when Jesus died, and yet, Jesus now calls them by a name that is more intimate than any He had used in His earthly life: "My brothers."

Although the term "My brothers" denotes pardon for their lack of faith, this term conveys still more. With these words, "My brothers", Jesus pulls them to His strong arms and shares all of His love with them. No greater gift of grace can come to a person than to be called by Jesus "My Brothers, My Sisters".

The words of the old hymn "Joyful, Joyful We Adore Thee" are appropriate.

Thou are giving and forgiving, Ever blessing, ever blest.

Wellspring of the joy of living, Ocean depth of happy rest!

Thou our father, Christ our brother, All who live in love are thine,

Teach us how to love each other, Lift us to the joy divine.

On this early Easter morning, as it were, when we consider matters of life and death, I remember my two brothers, who have gone on to the Church Triumphant lifted to the Joy Divine. I am also reminded of my sisters and brothers in this church and beyond who have also been called home. How I miss them all. You know that sense of emptiness and grief.

However, the Lord of resurrection speaks tenderly to us, while it is still dark: "Fear not. Fear not. You are my brother. You are my sister. I have forgiven your failures and your sins and I have destroyed death's dominion over you in my glorious resurrection. I will keep all the Saints in my care till you join the entire heavenly family." What a glorious day that will be—your day of resurrection.

Fear not, Brother. Fear not, Sister. The early morning is here.

Appreciating the Ascension
Acts 1: 1-11

A minister was frantically trying to complete his sermon late on Saturday night. His daughter came in, looked at him, looked at his manuscript, and then said, "Dad, does God tell you what to say?"

The minister thought for a while and then said, "Well, yes."

The daughter replied, "If God tells you what to say, why have you scratched so many things out?"

There are many scratch marks on my manuscript this morning, and I do not know how much of it comes from the Lord, but I trust that with your perseverance and God's help, we will learn something together.

During His early days of ministry in Galilee, Jesus, after teaching and healing the crowds, would often withdraw to a mountaintop to pray. On one occasion, Peter, James and John accompanied Him to a high mountain, and, while Jesus prayed, the veil of His humanity was swept aside. During this transfiguration, the awe-struck disciples saw the radiance of the eternal son of God.

In Matthew's gospel we read that the risen Christ met His followers once again on a mountaintop in Galilee and commissioned them with these words: "Go, therefore, and make disciples of all nations, baptizing them in the name of the Father and of the Son and of the Holy Spirit; and lo I am with you always."

One might assume that his great commission was the end of the gospel narrative. However, Luke writes to Theophilus in Acts of the Apostles and shares another mountaintop experience. Forty days after the resurrection, Jesus met His disciples on the Mount of Olives, a small hill outside the gates of Jerusalem. One can look down from it and see all of Jerusalem spread out below. From the Mount of Olives one can look at the countryside of Judea. In the distance stand the high mountains of Samaria, while far across the Jordan valley the mountaintops of Noab can be seen, truly the uttermost part of the earth.

While the disciples enjoyed this panoramic view, Jesus said, "You shall be my witnesses in Jerusalem and in Judea and in Samaria and to the ends of the earth."

When Jesus had said these words, according to Luke, He was lifted up and a cloud took Him out of their sight. We say it this way in the Apostles' Creed: "He ascended into Heaven and sitteth on the right hand of the Father almighty."

The ascension is one of the profound truths of Christian theology, and it has an important place in all the creeds of the Church. However, we in the Reformed Church often neglect it in our preaching. We seldom celebrate Ascension Day as we do Easter and Pentecost. According to the Church calendar, last Thursday was the fortieth day after the resurrection, and thus was Ascension Day.

The New Testament makes it quite clear that the ascension was an integral part of the early Christian thought. In the fourth Gospel, we find these words of our Lord, "What if you were to see the Son of man ascending where he was before?" And in the same Gospel, Jesus said to Mary Magdalene, "Do not cling to me, for I have not yet ascended to the Father."

In the New Testament epistles there are unmistakable references to the ascension. In Paul's letter to the Ephesians we read these words: "He who descended is also who ascended high above the heavens." In the first letter to Timothy there is a portion of an early Christian hymn which speaks of Jesus in this way. "He was manifested in the flesh, vindicated in the Spirit, seen by angels, believed on in the world, taken up in glory."

Although the doctrine of the ascension had a vital place in the teaching of the early church, people living in a modern age, in a space age, sometimes have great difficulty with this concept of the ascension. In Act 1:11, Luke describes the ascension with a Greek word, *analam-*

ephths, which means "to lift up." Some people have problems today with that terminology, because Luke thought in terms of a three-story universe in which the earth was in the middle, heaven was high above the sky and therefore literally upwards, and hades was beneath the earth and literally downwards. Thus, to Luke, Jesus ascended, that is He went above the sky into heaven, or into the abode of God.

What does a three-story universe concept do to our theology today when we know so much about the universe which scientists tell us is infinite? Several years ago *National Geographic* reported on the flight of Pioneer 10 to the planet Jupiter. From Jupiter, Pioneer 10 soared at great speeds headlong toward the Red Star, Aldebaran. The reporter for that magazine said that it will take 1,700,000 years for Pioneer 10 to reach that Red Star in the constellation Taurus. With such knowledge about the universe, do we believe that Jesus ascended into some ethereal place far beyond Aldebaran where He is millions of years away from us?

John A. T. Robinson wrote a classic about sixty years ago entitled *Honest to God*. Robinson had these words to say. "Most of us still retain, deep down, the mental image of God in the sky. We may have accepted the Copernican revolution in science, but yet still think in some ways of our Father in the heavens."

How do we explain the ascension and maintain our integrity about the universe? I think that Luke shares with us two very important facts in his accounts of the resurrection and the ascension. On Easter morning, the two women came to the tomb, looking for the crucified body of Jesus. They did not find His body, but they did see two men standing there in dazzling apparel.

These men asked the women, "Why do you seek the living among the dead?" In the first chapter of Acts, Luke reports that as Jesus ascended, a cloud took him out of their sight, and two men in white robes said to the disciples: "Men of Galilee, why do you stand here looking into heaven?"

Perhaps we, with the help of Luke's writings, can see that we often look for God in the wrong places, in tombs, and in the sky. According to these two men dressed in dazzling apparel, one will not find God in either place. So, we must not approach the ascension in spatial terms.

Obviously the scriptures teach us about the transcendence of God but time and space cannot contain Him. He is beyond both. The scriptures also clearly teach the imminence of God. Through the coming of the Holy Spirit at Pentecost, Christ fulfilled His promise. "Lo, I am with you always." Or as John of Patmos says in his Revelation, "The dwelling of God is with humans."

Attempting to ascertain where Jesus ascended is to miss the meaning of the ascension. It is not Luke's picture which is important, but rather the truth behind the picture.

On this Ascension Sunday, what do we find in Luke's account that somehow will add meaning and hope to our daily living? Karl Barth has written in his book *Credo* that "The ascension is the visible exaltation of God's Son."

The Apostle Paul says it a little differently. Christ Jesus, though He was in the form of God, did not count equality with God, a thing to be grasped. And being obedient to death, even the death of the cross, "God has highly exalted Him and bestowed upon Him the name that is above every name, that at the name of Jesus every knee should bow and every tongue confess that Jesus Christ is Lord."

In other words, the ascension is God's reversal of the sentence that the world imposed on His Son. Death had not done its worst, and the ascension is the enthronement of Christ after the humiliation of the cross.

In the first sermon that he preached after the ascension, Peter said, "This Jesus God raised up, and of that we are witnesses. He has been exalted at the right hand of God." And in Peter's first epistle we read these words, "Jesus Christ has gone into heaven, and is at the right hand of God with angels, authorities and powers subject to Him."

Martin Luther once said that the right hand of God is everywhere—active reigning Lord of the world. John Calvin wrote in his *Institutes*, "The right hand of God is not meant to designate a place rather it refers to the fact that Jesus Christ has been given a definite function in His ascension and exaltation, namely that of the exercise of divine power."

The ascension is Luke's way of saying that evil has been conquered and will continue to be conquered, because Jesus Christ is Lord of heaven and of earth.

As the hymnist says, "This is my Father's world." God's Son reigns over that world, and we rejoice on this Ascension Sunday that our destiny is in His hands and not in the hands of the principalities and powers of this crazy world.

There is another consequence of the ascension which we may grasp and understand only dimly. Emil Brunner has written in his book *The Christian Doctrine of Creation and Redemption*:

> In the person of the ascended Lord, humanity has entered heaven. He who sits at the right hand of God is the God-man. He is, therefore, our advocate who takes our part and speaks for us.

In the letter to the Church of Rome, Paul says, "It is Christ who sits at the right hand of God and intercedes for us."

The writer of the letter to the Hebrews has this to say, "He appears in the presence of God on our behalf."

Jesus Christ ascended into heaven not to end his work for mankind, but to continue it. The Larger Catechism teaches us,

> Christ makes intercession for us by appearing in our nature continually before the Father in heaven, in the merit of His obedience, declaring His will to have it applied to all believers, answering all accusations against us and procuring for us access to the throne of grace and acceptance by God.

During the Last Supper, Jesus said to Peter, "Simon, behold Satan has demanded to have you, but I have prayed for you that your faith may not fail." The ascended Lord prays for each one of us, for He is our great High Priest who is able to sympathize with every way we have yet without sinning. Knowing the weakness of human flesh, He prays constantly to the Father, and He stands before the Father in our human flesh, as our advocate, as someone on our side, allowing us to enter the presence of God.

Finally, the ascension is the act by which the church becomes the body of Christ on earth. Even though the risen Lord ascends into heaven and takes His flesh with Him, He continues to come to the world and to those in need through your flesh and through mine. We become the earthly body of Jesus. At the ascension, Christ gave to His followers the responsibility and privilege of completing His work here on earth.

Shortly before the crucifixion, Jesus said to His disciples, "Truly, truly I say to you he who believes in me will also do the works that I do and greater than these will he do because I go to the Father."

As they gathered on the Mount of Olives, the disciples asked Jesus if it were time to consummate His kingdom: "Lord, will you restore the Kingdom of Israel at this time?"

Jesus responded by saying "You shall be my witnesses in Jerusalem, in Judea, in Samaria, and to the ends of the earth."

Someone has pointed out that if Jesus had not ascended the disciples would never have realized that they were to be Christ's eyes, looking in compassion on all the suffering in the world. They were to be His hands, ministering to all in need. They were to be His feet, rescuing people from sin and despair and they were to be His lips, telling the world of His mercy and love.

Last fall a minister friend came home and preached a homecoming sermon. He is minister of one of the big Lutheran churches in Florida and also helps the Synod in the area of evangelism. He said that at the time he had his heart attack he was taken to coronary care. He tried to remain brave and to be positive for the sake of his family.

After his family had gone for the night, he became lonely, and realized the depth of his fears and of his pain and that truly he might not be able to accomplish all that he had wished to do.

About two o'clock in the morning, the nurse came in with her flashlight, as nurses often do, and she saw that he was crying. She said, "Pastor, what's the matter with you?"

He responded, "I know that I am a minister and I know that I should not be afraid, but I am."

She took his hand and said, "Well, let's pray the Lord's prayer." The point he was trying to make was that he gained a new concept of evangelism. Sometimes it is important simply to be present with people, to be the body of Christ standing along beside people who are hurting and who are afraid, literally being the mouth and the eyes and the hands and the feet of the ascended Lord.

Christ has ascended, but His body still remains through you and through me. Ascension Sunday is a grand day in the life of the church. Luke tells us that the disciples left the Mount of Olives with joy, and we too go out in joy—joy that Christ is at the right hand of God reigning over all the universe. Joy that He appears before the Father daily in our flesh as our advocate. Joy that He has left us to be His body, His witnesses here on earth.

Eastertide

2008

Two men walked Sunday evening to Emmaus from Jerusalem. As they walked, Jesus drew near and walked with them, but they did not recognize Him. Jesus asked "What are you talking about?"

The one named Cleopas asked, "Are you the only one who does not know what has happened these last few days?" So they tell the story. Then Jesus tells them a story, Jesus explains the Scriptures to them. As they come to Emmaus, they invite this apparent stranger to eat with them. Jesus took the bread and broke it. They eyes were opened, but He then disappeared.

So Cleopas and the other follower of Jesus returned to Jerusalem at once with the thrilling news that they had recognized the risen Lord when He opened their eyes through the breaking of bread. The journey was not far, just seven miles, so the two could easily retrace their steps, probably arriving around nine o'clock in the evening.

Two facts are noteworthy: they knew where to go to find the disciples, and they found them all gathered in one place, except for Judas Iscariot, who had hanged himself. This is what the morning news of the resurrection had accomplished in spite of the disbelief with which it was received. When Mary Magdalene rushed back to the city in the morning mist to report her discovery, she found only Peter and John. These two friends were still together. The rest were scattered.

But now on Sunday night, they were all together again. Since Jesus was dead, the bond appeared broken. Nothing could hold the eleven together. But when news came that our Lord was alive, the old bond resurfaced and they assembled in the upper room.

Jubilant shouts greeted the two late arrivals: "The Lord is risen, " they said. Luke tells us that as Cleopas and the other follower began to tell the eleven what had happened to them at Emmaus, Jesus suddenly stood in their midst and spoke to them. "Shalom. Peace be with you."

When we try to reconstruct this scene, we notice in John's Gospel that the doors were locked for fear of the Jews; thus, no one could have entered the room without first knocking and being admitted.

From Mark's Gospel we learn that the disciples were reclining on their couches at supper and the evening meal was apparently over. Those gathered in the room are engaged in conversation about all the things that had been reported concerning the resurrection of their

Lord. Suddenly, Jesus stood in their midst, having passed through the barred doors and strong walls, as if they were not there.

In his risen and glorified state, time, space, the stone of the tomb, the walls and doors of the buildings no longer impede the body of Jesus. He appears where he desires to appear, and his visible presence disappears when he desires to do so—truly a supernatural, incomprehensible reality to us.

Suddenly, standing in the midst, Jesus the risen Lord speaks, "Peace be with you." This peace is knowing that death is finally conquered through Christ's resurrection. This Hebrew greeting, Shalom, is always received with the same response: Shalom. Yet, the disciples make no response—for Luke tells us that they were terrified and afraid, thinking that they had seen a ghost.

The disciples had gathered in the Upper Room because they believed the reports of the resurrection, but when the risen Lord suddenly stood in the room in front of their eyes, the effect of the appearance terrified them. Their feelings were reminiscent of the terror they experienced when they were out on the Sea of Galilee in a raging storm when they suddenly spied Jesus walking on the water; and they cried out in fear, supposing that Jesus was a ghost.

The same experience occurs here, except no one cried out or said anything. And then, the risen Lord spoke to them: "Why are you afraid? See my hands and feet that it is I? Handle me, and see; for a ghost does not have flesh and bones."

Now this statement of our Lord evokes all kinds of questions regarding the state of resurrection, especially our resurrection. Perhaps a believer needs to turn at this point to the theology of the Apostle Paul, who learned much from Luke when the beloved physician was at his side.

In his first letter to the Corinthians Paul asked this question. "With what kind of body are the dead raised?" The apostle then gives us an answer: "In the old creation, you and I have physical bodies that we now know in the flesh. But in the new creation, in the new heaven and earth, we will be raised with spiritual bodies."

To enable his readers to understand the concept of a spiritual body, the apostle uses the analogy of a seed. Those who worked the earth for a living in Paul's day and those who work gardens today can appreciate this image. Paul seems to elaborate on the teachings of Jesus: a grain of wheat must fall in the ground and die and when it does, a beautiful green stalk grows majestically from the ground. Both a body and a seed are buried and something entirely different comes forth.

Strictly speaking, we know that a seed does not die if the power of germination remains. However, this was not the attempt of the apostle to describe a natural process nor did Paul believe that a dead body had the power of germination from which another body could grow.

What the apostle was trying to say in his analogy is that the resurrection is like a seed falling into the ground and coming forth with a different kind of body.

It is a sown seed, and it comes forth a fruitful stalk. We die and our bodies are buried. Our physical bodies decay but God gives us a new body, a spiritual body that is fit for our existence in the heavenly kingdom.

The Apostle confirms that there is no comparison between the physical body and the spiritual body. He says that the physical body dies in its perishableness and dishonor and weakness but the spiritual body is imperishable in its glory and power. And that is the Good News for the sinful, sickly, weak, distorted nature that you and I know in the flesh is destroyed by death.

In the Apostles' Creed, you and I affirm our faith by saying, "I believe in the resurrection of the body." The key to understanding this statement of faith is the fact that, for the Biblical writers, "body" was synonymous with "person". To say that we believe in the resurrection of the body is to believe that the human beings we are will live again. We will not be someone or something different from what we are now. We will be ourselves.

It was impossible for the Biblical writers to think of a person without a body. It is a person's body which makes him or her distinct and identifiable. For the Biblical writer to say that we will be the same persons in heaven that we are now he had to talk in terms of the resurrection of the body. The Biblical writers knew, as well as we, that physical bodies decompose and return to dust after death. But these writers were attempting to say that we do not lose our personal identity in death and that, at the resurrection, we shall possess whatever corresponds to our bodies in this present world that which makes us who we are as individual and distinct persons, with the ability to know God and each other.

Thus Jesus says to the awe-stricken disciples, "Do not be afraid, it is I. See my hands and feet." John adds in his Gospel our Lord's side namely, the wound that had been inflicted by the slash of the spear. Thus he holds out his hands and his feet and as John adds, his side. "It is I, the Jesus you have known." Our Lord establishes his personal identity by means of a body: hands, feet, side. These bear the five holy wounds of his crucifixion. By them, the disciples know him to be the risen savior.

Here one sees the grace of God bountiful as it is! In our resurrection, we do not retain the scars and suffering of life. All are removed for us in the resurrection for as John says in his Revelation: "I saw a new heaven and a new earth and the sea was no more." (The sea for the Jews was that which represented the human's greatest fear perpetuated by the Phoenicians who kept competition out of the shipping lanes by fabricating tales of great sea monsters.)

And John continues, "And God shall wipe away every tear from their eyes and there shall be no more death, neither sorrow not crying. Neither shall there be any more pain for the former things are passed away."

In the resurrection, our spiritual bodies will be perfect and free from the scars of earth. Not so with the glorified savior. He retains his scars for two reasons. First, seated at the right hand of the Father, he shows his scars constantly so that the Godhead will always know what it is like for you and me to live this earthly life of suffering. And God's grace reacts to those scars by covering ours.

Second, the risen Lord retains his scars in the resurrection so that earth and heaven will always recognize him for the sacrifice he made for us: dying on a cross, covering our sins with his cleansing blood, and rising from the dead that we might rise in Him.

The most interesting part of this passage is that Jesus asked, "Do you have something to eat?" And they gave him a piece of broiled fish and He ate it before them. This evokes an interesting question. Does God eat food and shall we in the heavenly kingdom?

Remember the story of Abraham and Sarah preparing a meal for God and His angels? God needs no nourishment. Neither will our spiritual bodies. But one of the things that the communion table symbolizes for us each Lord's Day is that eating and drinking with Jesus symbolizes eternal fellowship with Christ.

At each celebration of the Lord's Supper, I try to remind us that our Lord has prepared a special place at His heavenly banquet table where you and I will sup with Him forever. Jesus takes the broiled fish and eats it to show the startled disciples, and us, that death has not destroyed our fellowship with Him. Resurrection guarantees it forever.

Finally, we wrestle with the question that we all ask in our minds. "When does the resurrection take place? Does it occur immediately at death or only at the fulfillment of history?"

To Martha, Jesus said, "I am the resurrection and the Life. He who believes in me, though he were dead yet shall he live. And whoever lives and believes in me shall never die."

To the dying thief, Jesus said, "Today, you will be with me in Paradise."

In his letter to the Romans, Paul writes: "If God is for us, who can be against us? Who shall separate us from the love of Christ? For, I am persuaded that neither death nor life can separate us from the love of God in Christ Jesus our Lord."

So the answer of Christ and His Apostle is this: When we breathe our last, we immediately awake. We immediately are held and lifted up to the presence of the risen Lord.

The Roman historian, Pliny, described a Christian funeral this way, "They follow his body rejoicing as though he was going from one place to another."

That we do, immediately, in the twinkling of an eye, at the sound of the trumpet and we are raised because Christ is risen. He is risen indeed and so are we.

And now may the God of Grace, who has called us into His glory by Christ Jesus, be glory and dominion forever and ever.

The City for the Risen

Mark 16: 1-16

Revelation 21: 1-5; 10-12; 16-18; 22-23

The night began like most nights for a retired couple. After a hearty evening meal, Joe and Ruth, parents of my wife's best friend in high school and college, sat together in their small cozy den, carefully carrying out their evening ritual. Sitting in the reclining chair with his feet lazily propped up, Joe carefully studied the obituary column on the front page of the evening paper, and then he turned and slowly digested the box scores of all the baseball games on the previous day. Ruth, with her "Ben Franklin spectacles" perched halfway down her nose, slowly stitched a hole in Joe's shirt. Trying to make conversation over the troublesome television, Ruth managed to get a grunt or two out of her husband who laboriously lost himself in the evening print.

Midway through the eleven o'clock news, the tired pair decided to retire for the night after the weatherman had promised that the dreary weather would end with the rising of the sun. Why should they stay up for the sports report? Joe had spent the entire evening solicitously studying all the box scores.

After kissing each other good night, Joe and Ruth simultaneously turned out their reading lamps on the night stands and snuggled up together, hoping for a restful and refreshing night of sleep. Suddenly the stillness of the night was interrupted by Joe's snoring and Ruth lay awake, anxiously thinking about her children and grandchildren.

As she tirelessly tossed and turned, did she imagine that she heard footsteps outside of her window? Rising to her elbows, she quietly listened for further evidence, as her thumping heart drowned out all other noise. Slowly easing her head back down to the pillow, she curled up closer to Joe and silently said to herself the words of Psalm 121, "He will not suffer thy foot to be moved: he that keepeth thee will not slumber. Behold he that keepeth Israel shall neither slumber not sleep.'"

Unfortunately, Ruth's imagination was not playing tricks on her. The nocturnal intruder suddenly kicked in the glass of the kitchen storm door, and he was wildly jimmying the lock on the back door. By this time, both Ruth and Joe were sitting straight up in the bed. Ruth reached for the phone to call the police, and Joe fumbled around in the drawer of the night stand, searching for the revolver he recently purchased after several robberies had occurred in the neighborhood. Like Barney Fife, Joe loaded his one bullet into the chamber, praying that he would not have to shoot anyone.

Although it seemed like hours, the police arrived in a matter of minutes. They quickly apprehended the intruder without any incident. High on drugs, this frightening interloper thought he was at his estranged girl friend's house.

As the police questioned the couple and filled out their report, Joe suddenly grew pale. He complained about the tightness in his chest and the shortness of breath. Suddenly his knees buckled, and Joe lay motionlessly on the floor. His heart had stopped beating. While one policeman summoned an ambulance, the other administered cardiopulmonary resuscitation. Momentarily the policeman revived Joe, but en route to the hospital, the ambulance attendant had to shock Joe's heart on two different occasions. The doctors had to carry out the same procedure in the emergency room and in the cardiac care unit the next day.

Several days later, Joe's younger daughter, who has been my wife's best friend for many years, visited with her father alone. He weakly grabbed her hand, and said, "Elaine, you must promise me one thing. If my heart stops beating again, you must not allow them to shock me. I have seen heaven. It is the most beautiful sight that I have ever seen. The city is pure gold, and I am ready to take my place there."

Elaine and the family honored Joe's wishes. Several days later Joe's heart stopped, and he quietly and joyfully embraced his citizenship in the heavenly city.

Those words of Joe intrigued me, and I want us to spend a few moments on this Easter morn thinking about them: "If my heart stops beating again, you must not allow them to shock me. I have seen heaven. It is the most beautiful sight that I have ever seen. The city is pure gold, and I am ready to take my place there."

Joe's words are not the words of a psychotic visionary. They are words of a devout believer in Jesus Christ.

I believe the words of Joe just as I believe the words of all those persons whom Dr. Kuebler Ross reports in her book, *On Death and Dying*, and the words of those persons whom Dr. Moody reports in his book, *Life After Life*. I find great comfort in the testimony of a friend who witnessed to the reality of resurrection and to the truth of the heavenly city which John of Patmos saw in his vision. I find great joy in the testimony of one who affirms through experience that Scripture teaches immediately upon death God welcomes His children as citizens of His heavenly city.

I realize that one finds much disagreement and debate among physicians and theologians regarding this heavenly phenomena. Reason tells us that we can seek to explain these experiences in terms of psychological trauma. Understandably, one can argue over semantics: How can we consider someone clinically dead when he/she still registers brain waves? We can logically laugh at the lunacy of these accounts, but what we cannot do is to dismiss this phenomena altogether.

I believe the words of Joe. I believe that God momentarily released him from time and space, allowing him to see the city of heaven which awaits you and me. Realizing that time and space have no meaning when we escape these physical confinements, one can see much and travel great distances, as it were, in a matter of earthly seconds. As Peter writes in his Second Epistle, "But beloved, be not ignorant of this one thing, that one day is with the Lord as a thousand years, and a thousand years as one day" (3:8)

Call me "psychotic," if you wish. Call me a hopeless romantic who is grasping at straws, if you must. You will not hurt my feelings. I believe Joe, I also believe that when you and I who are in Christ face death, we too, shall immediately take our place in the heavenly city, because I believe in Christ's Easter victory.

Prior to His crucifixion and resurrection, our Lord ministered to His fearful followers with these words: "Let not your heart be troubled: ye believe in God, believe also in me. In my Father's house are many mansions: if it were not so, I would have told you. I go to prepare a place for you. And if I go and prepare, a place for you, I will come again, and receive you unto myself; that where I am, there ye may be also. And now I have told you before it comes to past, that when it comes to pass, ye might believe." (John 14: 1-3; 21; 29KJV)

The words and experience of Joe merely reflect the Lord's teaching. In the Father's house, His dwelling place, one will find many mansions. Through His resurrection, Jesus has entered the heavenly city to prepare a place for us. If it were not so He, who is Truth, would have told us.

From Joe's experience, we can discern very little about the heavenly city other than it was the most beautiful sight that he had ever seen, and that he was willing to sacrifice perhaps further years of life with his wife, children and grandchildren in order to immediately enter that eternal and ethereal city.

On this Easter morn, we celebrate God's victory in the resurrection of our Lord Jesus Christ. As we rejoice in God's triumph over the powers of evil and death, and as our thoughts turn toward the resurrection, we begin to wonder what life in heaven will be like when Christ's resurrection becomes ours. What will we see and what will we experience when we walk triumphantly into the heavenly city of God? One may doubt the reliability of Joe's description of that city of beauty, but can one truthfully doubt the words of Holy Writ which reveal John's vision of the heavenly city.

I have told you something about Joe's life, but nothing of John's. Who was John? We cannot say with certainty. Some scholars believe he was John, the beloved Apostle. Others say that his form of writing differs too much from the Gospel and the Epistles, and thus, we cannot identify him as the one who at the Last Supper reclined "in Jesus' bosom." The true identity of John has little consequence for us this morning. All that matters is that he was a believer in the risen Christ, and because of his belief he was exiled to the island of Patmos during a time of great persecution, perhaps during the reign of the Roman emperor Domitian in A.D. 96.

During this time of exile, God allowed John to see through a vision something of the eternal. Although John employs much symbolism in the description of his vision, we can, on this resurrection morn, make—with certainty—a few statements about the quality of resurrected life.

The first thing that John enables us to see through his vision is that heaven is a city: "And I saw a new city, new Jerusalem, coming down out of heaven from God." John tells us that we shall live in a city when we enter the heavenly kingdom of God.

I recommend to you for further reading about life in the heavenly city, Dr. Guthrie's book, *Christian Doctrine*.

"We do not have to look forward to an eternal life of isolated loneliness as pictured in the typical cartoon of a man sitting all by himself on his little private cloud in a vast empty sky. Nor can we think of a lazy pastoral scene in which there is nothing to do but lie around in bored idleness. The Bible chooses rather the picture of city life. A city is a place where there is work to be done, where there is excitement and action, where new building and new ways of doing things are always in progress." He continues,

> It is a complex, cosmopolitan place where all kinds of people, of different races, classes, and nationalities have to learn to live together, depend on each other, cooperate with each other, and be responsible to and for each other. On the other hand, a city is a place where there is room for real individuality.
>
> That is what the City of God will be like. It will be a creative, dynamic moving from perfection to perfection in which there will always be new things to learn, new things

to do, new tasks to perform—under the God whose own perfection is not static and lifeless, but the perfection of the God who will always be a living active Creator.(page 393)

I find it absolutely exciting to realize that heavenly life is a form of city life with the chance to make friendships with all the saints, with the chance to learn all the mysteries of God, and with the chance to perform all the vocations of God's heavenly city. I hope that I can finally learn carpentry there.

One must not lose sight of the Easter implication. Since heavenly life is a city of life, Christians cannot run from the problems and the opportunities of living and working with all the different kinds of people in urban life. It is our eternal future.

The second thing that John enables us to see through his vision is that in the heavenly city there is no temple: "And I saw no temple in the city, for its temple is the Lord God Almighty and the Lamb." I am sure that it is encouraging to you to know that we will not have to spend an eternity singing strange hymns and listening to long, boring sermons.

There is no temple or church in the heavenly city because that city has no need of one. The Lord God Almighty and the Lamb dwell in the midst of her, and the citizens of the heavenly city all know God and His ways.

Once again, we find for ourselves an Easter implication. Since the Church does not exist in the heavenly city because all citizens know the Almighty and the Lamb, then we, the Easter people must realize that our church does not exist only for us We live for all the people in this city and in the world because the Bible tells that "God so loved the world that He gave His only Son." Thus it is imperative that we as a church live and work for others through word and deed that they may come to know Jesus Christ, and, thus enjoy the eternal life of this heavenly city.

Finally, through the symbolism of John, we can say several things about the heavenly city and the quality of life in it. However, one must cautiously guard against pushing this symbolism too far.

John tells us that the heavenly city is so beautiful that words cannot describe it. Those, like Joe, who have momentarily died and have caught a glimpse of that city do not want to return to this body of flesh, and when they do, they are ready to forsake all, even their closest relationships, to return to it. John says that the holy city radiates with the glory of God like rare jewels and precious gold. Its beauty beckons us.

John goes on to say that the heavenly city is fifteen hundred miles long, i.e., it is large enough for all people of all ages who want to eternally live with God and the Lamb. In the city, one finds no need for the sun, moon, or artificial light because the brilliance of God's glory illumines the entire city, chasing away the darkness of night and the darkness of evil.

The heavenly city, according to John, is surrounded by a high wall, "And the city has no need of sun or moon to shine on it, for the glory of God is its light, and its lamp is the Lamb. The nations will walk by its light, and the kings of the earth will bring their glory into it." Rev. 21: 23-24 and Rev. 21:12.

It is a secure place to live, and because one lives securely in that city, he/she never has to fear death or pain, nor does one ever have to endure sorrow, sickness or tears. The earthly burdens and struggles have no place in the heavenly city and that is good news for those who constantly wrestle with day to day problems.

One can dismiss the words of Joe, "I have seen heaven. It is the most beautiful sight that I have ever seen. The city is pure gold, and I am ready to take my place there."

Yet one cannot dismiss the word of God which comes to us through the vision of an exiled believer in Christ. "And I, John, saw the holy city, new Jerusalem, coming down from God out of heaven, prepared as a bride adorned for husband."

Neither can one dismiss the promise of the Eternal Christ. "In my Father's dwelling place, there are many mansions. If it were not so, I would have told you. I go to prepare a place for you, and if I go, I will come again and receive you unto myself, that where I am you may be also."

The Easter hope is certain. God in Christ has destroyed the shackles of death. Now we know that a perfect life awaits us in the heavenly city. With great anticipation, we wait for our new citizenship because Christ is risen.

Prayer

Thanks be to you, O God, for Your Easter victory. Thanks be to You, O Lord, for our victorious Christ. Give to us Your comforting peace as we live each day, not knowing when Your call to the heavenly city may come. As we live and wait, may our earthly city and church reflect the quality of life which shall be ours in the new Jerusalem, through Jesus Christ, our risen Lord.

The Spirit of Pentecost
Acts 2:1-15
Mark 6:45-52

Jesus and the disciples came to the end of a long, tiring day. The crowd of people pressed against the Master and his followers, hungry for healing and hope. As the sun began to set, several of the disciples said to the Savior, "Send the crowds away so they may go into the villages and buy food for themselves." But Jesus said, them, "They need not go away; you give them something to eat."

The disciples answered, "We have nothing here but five loaves and two fishes." So Jesus said, "Bring them here to me." Ordering the crowds to sit down on the grassy knoll, Jesus blessed the bread and fish and fed over 5,000 people. When all had eaten, there were twelve baskets of bread left over.

As the day of miracles ended, Jesus told the disciples to get into the boat and to sail to the other side of the Sea of Galilee while he dismissed the crowds. As the disciples journeyed across the water and the multitude marched home, Jesus went up on a mountain—alone—to pray. As our Lord prayed, the disciples struggled, seeking to steer the tiny boat through a sudden storm that surprised them. The waves battered the brittle boat and they made little headway, for as Matthew says, "The wind was against them."

Realizing that his followers were in trouble, Jesus came to them in their distress, walking on the water. When the anxious disciples saw Jesus walking on the sea, their anxiety turned into fear, crying out, "It is a ghost!" However, Jesus allayed their fears saying, "Do not be afraid, it is I."

Peter, the impetuous one, said, "Lord, if it is you, bid me come to you on the water." Jesus, standing on the sea, said, "Come!" So Peter stepped out of the boat, stood on the waves and walked toward Jesus.

But as the strong winds howled across the stormy sea, Peter's heart filled with fear and he began to sink! Desperately he cried to the Savior, "Lord, save me."

Immediately Jesus reached out his hand and caught Peter, saying to him, "You of little faith, why did you doubt?" As Jesus and Peter, hand in hand, stepped into the boat together, the winds and waves became calm and those in the boat worshiped the Savior, "Truly you are the Son of God."

Here ends the first of two Bible stories I want to tell you this morning. In this first one, I want you to concentrate on these five words: "The wind was against them." From personal experience, we know that the wind can often be against us. If you do not know that, you will before your life is done, and the older a person becomes, the more he or she realizes that much of life is lived against the wind. Sometimes the events of life cause us to feel that we take one step forward and two backwards. The wind is against us, always threatening to undo our plans and hope and dreams! At times it takes an enormous amount of energy just to stay where you are and not lose ground, not to fall back, to hold on.

As the disciples were rowing for dear life, making little headway against the wind, Jesus came to them walking on water and they were terrified. It is at this point that the story asks its most piercing question of you and me: Do you and I believe that at the darkest and most exhausting places in our lives that we will find strength and peace to see us through?

Now I want to share with you a second Bible story that is the account of Pentecost.

Fifty days after Easter and ten days after Jesus ascended into heaven, the followers of Jesus were gathered together in one place. And suddenly from heaven there came a sound like the rush of a mighty wind and it filled the entire house where they were sitting. Divided tongues of fire appeared in their midst, and a tongue rested on all of them. All of the disciples were filled with the Holy Spirit and began to speak in other languages as the Spirit gave them the ability. And all who had gathered in Jerusalem for the feast of Pentecost heard the gospel of Jesus Christ spoken in their tongue.

Now in the first Bible story, I asked you to concentrate on these five words "the wind was against them." In this second story I want you now to concentrate on these words, "There came a sound like the rush of a mighty wind."

The Hebrew word for "Spirit" is *rauch*, and *rauch* can be translated as "breath" or "wind." Thus, the Holy Spirit is none other than the Holy Rauch, the Holy Wind, the Holy Breath of Christ.

One of the first Bible stories you learned as a child was the creation of Adam. The writer of Genesis tells us that God breathed into Adam's nostrils the rauch or the "breath of life" and the first man became a living being.

On Pentecost, the ascended Christ returned to earth as the Holy Spirit—as the Holy Breath—as the Holy Wind—entering the hearts of the disciples and us all making us living beings forever.

Who is the Holy Spirit? The Holy Spirit is the holy breath of Christ, the rush of a holy wind which lives in us now.

Prior to his crucifixion, Jesus spoke these words to the disciples: "I will not leave you desolate. I will come to you. In that day, you will know that I am in my Father, and you in me and I in You. I am with you always." The Holy Spirit is the breath of Christ, the presence of Christ, the wind of Christ in you and me.

Now consider the wind of Christ in you. Jesus said, "You shall receive power when the Holy Spirit comes upon you." The Greek word for "power" is *duvameis*, whence comes our English word *dynamite*.

The Holy Spirit, the Holy Breath of Christ lives and dwells in you with power greater than dynamite, a power like the rush of a mighty wind.

Return with me to the first Bible story where the disciples struggled to survive in the tempest-tossed boat for the wind was against them. Across the surging sea came the encouraging words, "Be not afraid, I am here."

What the story of Jesus walking on water wants to know is this: will you and I let our fears defeat us? Fear can defeat us. Fear of being controlled. Fear of losing control. Fear of the future and wanting to control it knowing that we cannot control it. Worrying and asking, "What if this happens, what if that happens?" There is not one of us here this morning who does not face fear in his or her life.

"Take heart; be not afraid," Jesus said to Peter. Listen to the Savior's words, "be not afraid!" Peter wanted to believe that was true, but he was only half convinced, and so he said, "Lord, if it is you, bid me come to you on the water." Faith, after all, does not mean sitting on your hands. So Jesus said, "Come to me." Peter stepped out of the boat, started walking on the water, and came toward Jesus. But when Peter concentrated on the strength of the wind that was against him, he began to sink. You and I will never learn to live if we pay too much attention to all that is working against us. We will sink for sure! So Peter cried out, "Lord, save me."

The one thing I want you to remember is this: when the wind is against you, remember the rush of the mighty wind that is in you. When life becomes extremely difficult and it will, do not forget the

One who said, "Be not afraid," for the holy wind of Christ is in you and with you and over you, saying, "Peace, be still." The rush of the mighty wind is always greater than the wind that is against you. "Be not afraid," he says.

In the first Bible story, it was not the storm that sank Peter. It was his fear and his inability to believe in the sustaining presence of Christ in the midst of the storm. Desperate and unable to save himself, Peter grabbed the hand that Jesus offered, and when they stepped from the rolling waters into the boat, the wind that was against them ceased and the disciples worshiped Jesus saying, "Truly you are the Son of God."

"Truly you are the Son of God." Those are words to remember. Christ is always in the midst of the storm, when the wind is against us. This reality only faith can know. You and I can never do anything about life's difficult moments as this is the nature of our human existence. We can only do something about how we handle the dark, frightening, stormy days when fear can bring paralysis to our souls.

Faith is not the absence of fear. Faith is the courage to work through the fear, on the rolling, stormy waves, grasping the hand that is offered. To be courageous is not to be fearless. It is to be able to act in spite of fear.

Every day that you and I live, we must decide again which it will be for us, fear or faith.

Every day we must decide again whether or not we believe more deeply in the winds that blow against us or in the rush of a mighty wind that is in us.

There will come a time when the wind will be against us. It may be a time of facing deep loneliness and confusion and fear. In the darkest night, when the wind is against you, remember the rush of a mighty wind in you, even Jesus Christ who will not let you sink—Not Now—Not Ever.

A Dim Image in a Mirror: The Trinity
II Corinthians 13: 11-13

The church fathers consecrated the first Sunday after Pentecost to the mystery of the Trinity in 900 A.D. According to the Christian calendar, the cycle of redemption begins with the season of Advent, and concludes with Pentecost, which we celebrated last Sunday. Today, we Presbyterians join denominations all over this land and all around the world in the observance of Trinity Sunday. We do this to help us summarize the entire work of salvation in contemplation of God who is Father, Son, and Holy Spirit. Obviously the concept of three Persons in the Godhead is a mystery that no one can easily understand.

Saint Augustine said that he had written about the Trinity in order not to keep silent about it. Karl Barth has written these words in the first volume of his *Church Dogmatics*. "When we have said what is meant by Father, Son, and Holy Spirit, we must continue and say that we have said nothing." Yet, the doctrine of the Trinity is too important to the life and the theology of the church to be heedlessly accepted because the church tells us to, or to be casually tossed aside because no one can intelligently explain it.

When I wrestle with the mystery of the Trinity, I find much encouragement in the words of the Apostle Paul that were written in his first letter to Corinth. Paul says, "Now we see in a mirror dimly, but then face to face. Now I know in part; then I shall fully understand." These words of Paul may have little meaning for us, but they were very suggestive to the Corinthians. Corinth was a manufacturing center for mirrors. Unlike our modern mirror with its perfect reflection, the Corinthian mirror was made of highly polished metal, and even at its best, gave but an imperfect reflection. When one looked into a Corinthian mirror, he saw only a dim, shadowy reflection.

In this earthly life, according to Paul, we sometimes see only dim reflections of God and much of what we know about Him is mystery and riddle. However, Paul's confidence assures us that one day God will lift the veil from our eyes and we shall fully understand the mysterious. Until then, the concept of the triune God hovers over us like a dim image in a Corinthian mirror.

Yet, we continue to sing every Sunday morning, "Glory be to the Father, and to the Son, and to the Holy Ghost." In baptism, we hear the minister say, "I baptize you in the name of the Father, and of the Son, and of the Holy Spirit." At the close of the worship service, we often receive this familiar benediction, "The grace of our Lord Jesus

Christ, the love of God, and the communion of the Holy Spirit be with you all." Obviously, the Trinity has a very important part in the worship services of the church, but what does it mean to us? What does the Bible have to say about this doctrine?

Unfortunately, the Bible does not say anything specific about the Trinity. One can search from cover to cover and nowhere will he find in the Scriptures the word "Trinity," nor will he find the words, "God in three persons." Although we do not find the doctrine of the Trinity in the Bible, we do find statements about God which led the early church to formulate this teaching of the Trinity. Consider our text for today: "The grace of our Lord Jesus Christ, and the love of God, and the fellowship of the Holy Spirit be with you all." This text along with others forced the theologians of the early church to ask what relationship the Father had to the Son and what relationship the Son had to the Spirit. Therefore, this doctrine of the Trinity was an attempt by the early church to answer the question, "Who is God?"

As we consider the doctrine of the Trinity, we must emphasize the affirmation that there is but one God—not three. When those questioning Jesus asked the Shema—the ancient creed of Israel: "Hear, O Israel, the Lord our God, the Lord is one." The Apostle Paul reiterated the Lord's teaching of the one God when he wrote in his first letter to Corinth, "There is no God but one." In his Epistle to the Ephesians, Paul wrote, "There is one God and Father of us all."

Our ancestors in the Presbyterian Church of Scotland composed these words in their Confession of 1560: "We confess and acknowledge one God alone, to whom alone we must cleave, whom alone we must serve, whom only we must worship, and in whom alone we put our trust." So, biblical faith and the reformed tradition affirm the oneness of God.

Yet we find ourselves in a state of confusion when we confess the oneness of God, and then read the New Testament which seems to mention Jesus and God in the same breath. In John's Gospel, Thomas looks at the risen Christ and proclaims, "My Lord and my God." Right after the crucifixion John records these words of our Lord, "I and the Father are one, and he who has seen me has seen the Father." When we profess that God is present and known as Jesus of Nazareth, how do we avoid saying that there are, in fact, two Gods—one in heaven, and one who walked the street of Jerusalem?

The writers of the gospels and the writers of the epistles do not answer that question, but it appears that this kind of question and questions like it encouraged members of the early church to express their faith in one God through the doctrine of the Trinity.

The ancient language of the early church used to explain this doctrine may contribute to our misunderstanding of the Trinity today. Our own Westminster Confession of Faith describes the Trinity in this manner, "In the unity of the Godhead there are three Persons of one substance." As I work with communicants' classes, as I teach Sunday School classes, and as I talk with individuals about the meaning of the Trinity, I find that the language of the ancient church is often misleading. The words of Westminster Confession of Faith appear to suggest a tritheism rather than a oneness in the Godhead. Yet the writers of the Confession of Faith did not mean to imply that the

Father, Son and Holy Spirit are three different persons, three different Gods, who share somehow a common divine essence. Rather, those who framed the wording of this doctrine used the word "substance" to mean "same in being." So, we can paraphrase our Westminster Confession of Faith to say, "In the unity of the Godhead there are three Persons who are the same being." Or, we can say it another way, "The Father, Son and Holy Spirit are identical. They are the same God."

If this word "substance" (that is, in the unity of the Godhead there are three Persons of one substance) confuses us, what about the use of the phrase, "three Persons in the Godhead"? To talk about God in three Persons implies, for some people, that one finds in the Godhead three different personalities, three different Gods somehow combined into one. The church fathers never intended to leave us with that kind of understanding of the Trinity at this point. Using our modern day understanding of the word "person," we affirm that there are not three different personalities in God. Rather, God is one personality, one person, if you will, who is Father, who is Son, and who is Holy Ghost or Holy Spirit.

Now, to you this reasoning may sound like senseless or pretentious language designed to confuse. However, the church must use language to try to seek to communicate its understanding of God. The church fathers formulated the doctrine of the Trinity as a means of speaking about God, one person who is known and who works and lives in a threefold way: Father, Son, and Holy Spirit.

The formulators of the doctrine of the Trinity used the Latin word "persona" to express the three different ways in which God lives and works. Rachel Henderlite has been a big help to me in her book *A Call to Faith*. She tells us that "persona" in the early church referred to a mask worn by an actor in the theater to help him play his role. Later, that same "person" referred to the role itself, rather than to the mask. When the church fathers used the term "persona" or "person" in the doctrine of the Trinity, they intended to say something like this, "way of existence" or "way of being." And so, to say that God is three persons is to say that God has three ways of existence or three ways of being God.

In a few moments, we shall sing, "Holy, Holy, Holy, Lord God Almighty . . . God in three Persons, blessed Trinity." When we sing about God in three Persons, we are saying that God is one God who has three ways of existence. So, for me, the easiest way to define the Trinity is to say that God has three ways of being God—as Father, as Son, as Holy Spirit. We do not fall prey to the old heresy of Modalism when we define the Trinity as three ways of God being God, as long as we remember that God lives and works in three ways.

We must also remember that one cannot place any temporal succession to God's three ways of being God as if there were first the Father, long before creation, and then the Son at Bethlehem, and then the Holy Spirit at Pentecost. While God lived and worked as Father in creation, He also lived and worked as the eternal Son and as the Holy Spirit. In his letter to the Colossians, Paul wrote that Christ is the image of the invisible God. He is before all things and in Him all things were created. The writer of the Book of Genesis describes creation in this manner, "In the beginning God created the heavens and the earth. The earth was without form and void, and darkness was upon the face of the deep and the Spirit of God was moving across the face of the waters." God not only lived and worked as Father over His creation, but He also lived and worked as the Son and the Holy Spirit in creation. The gospel writer, John, expressed that same reality in this manner when he recorded the words of Jesus, "...and when Jesus had said this, He breathed on them and said, 'Receive the Holy Spirit.'" God lived and worked as the Son, while never ceasing to live and work as the Father and as the Holy Spirit.

I think that George S. Hendry says it best in his book, *The Westminster Confession for Today*, "In Christ we have God with us and in the Holy Spirit we have God in us without ever ceasing to have God over us." Hendry goes on to say that

> The purpose of the doctrine of the Trinity is to guard the basic Christian faith that in Christ and in the Holy Spirit we have God Himself. By the same token, that doctrine guards the unity of the works of God. It is not intended to point to a division of labor within the Godhead, as if the Father alone were responsible for creation, and the Son alone were responsible for redemption, and the Spirit alone were responsible for sanctification. No, the Father, the Son and the Spirit—one God does all.

The doctrine of the Trinity is often a confusing mystery. At times, trying to understand the Trinity is like looking at a dim, shadowy image in an old Corinthian mirror. Paul Tillich writes a very interesting thought about this doctrine of the Trinity in the third volume of his

Systematic Theology. He says, "The Trinity is the threefold manifestation of God as creative power, as saving love, and as ecstatic transformation."

The doctrine of the Trinity may be like a dim image in a mirror, but is it also the story of good news about the one God who loves us and who lives and works for us in three different ways. He is God the Father who willed and created us. He is God the Son who loved us enough to reconcile us to Himself and to one another. He is God the Holy Spirit who gives us the power to be what we were intended to be in the beginning.

Who is God? He is the one God who has three different ways of living and working as God—Father, Son and Holy Spirit. He has created us. He has redeemed us. He has empowered us to live as His children.

Prayer

And now unto God the Father, God the Son and God the Holy Spirit be ascribed by us and by all the church all praise and glory, dominion and power, now and forever. Amen.

Our Nation's Security
Psalm 33: 4-22

In his famous pamphlet, "The Crisis", Thomas Paine wrote the following words in December, 1776.

> These are the times that try men's souls.
> The summer soldier and the sunshine patriot
> will in this crisis, shrink from the service
> of his country; but he that stands it now,
> deserves the love and thanks of man and woman.
> Tyranny, like hell, is not easily conquered; yet we
> have this consolation with us, that the harder the
> conflict, the more glorious the triumph. What we
> obtain too cheap, we esteem too lightly.

George Washington had these bold words of Thomas Paine read

to his troops, and they encouraged the Continental Army during the darkest days of the war to fight fiercely and bravely for the precious cause of freedom.

Wednesday we celebrate our nation's year of independence. Remembering our past in an integral part of celebrating July 4th, and we thank God for people like Thomas Paine, George Washington, and all the men and women who courageously fought and died in order that we Americans may enjoy the rich legacy of living, working and worshipping in freedom.

However, our celebration of freedom calls us to consider our future as well as our past. How do we as a nation preserve and protect our privilege of living as a free people? How do we guarantee our children's children the same rights of freedom that we enjoy today? As Franklin said on the steps of Constitution Hall, "We have given you a republic, if you can keep it."

"These are the times that try our souls," as we look at America's future and as we debate the issues of national security. "These are the times that try our souls," because such discussions of national defense is vulnerable; and such discussions remind us of the horrible holocaust that can occur if we ever have to meet the enemy in a military confrontation. "These are the times that try our souls," because we are not quite sure what makes our nation secure.

As we prepare to observe Independence Day, I would like to suggest that we include a portion of Psalm 33 in our celebration. This psalm is a festival hymn that was sung during postexilic times when

God's people celebrated a national holiday. In this psalm, we discover three realities which make a nation secure.

The first reality which makes a nation secure is the Word of the Lord. Listen to these words of the psalmist.

> For the word of the Lord is upright; and all His work is done in faithfulness. He loves righteousness and justice; the earth is full of the steadfast love of the Lord. By the word of the Lord, the heavens were made, and all the host of them by the breath of his mouth He gathered the waters of the sea as in a battle; He puts the deeps in the storehouses. Let all the earth fear the Lord, let all the inhabitants of the world stand in awe of Him. For He spoke, and it came to be; He commanded and it stood forth.

In these six verses, one sees the dynamic power of the Word of God. According to the psalmist, God's word and work are the same creation and history. He speaks and something happens. As the author of Psalm 33 has written, "For God spoke, and it came to be. He commanded and it stood forth." The writer of Genesis said, "And God said, 'Let there be light.' And there was light." So we see that God's Word is so powerful that when He speaks, creation, life and redemption occur.

The psalmist emphasized that God's word and work are always grounded in goodness. He said it this way in verse four: "The Word of the Lord is upright; and all his work is done in faithfulness." The writer of Genesis put it this way: "And God saw that it was good."

In creation and in history, God works for good. He never swerves from his upright purposes. Righteousness, justice, faithfulness, and steadfast love are the fundamental essence of God and the world He created and sustains.

The God who created the world and who sustains the world through all ages by the power of His speech is the same God who created Israel as a nation by delivering her from slavery in Egypt and by establishing a covenant with her at Sinai. Once again God's word and work are the same. He spoke, and Israel was delivered. He spoke and Israel became His special nation.

Called by God's word into this intimate relationship with the Lord, Israel was obligated to express in all of her words and deeds what God had expressed in His creation and redemption.

The people of Israel were to express to each other and to other nations the goodness, the righteousness, the justice that they had experienced in God's word and work in God's calling and saving her from extinction. Therefore the people of Israel were to express that goodness and righteousness of God to others in their daily words and works.

The prophet Micah said, "What does the Lord require of thee, but to do justly, to love kindness, and to walk humbly with thy God." The security of a nation is found in the integrity of God's people.

Security is found in obeying the word and work of God. Security is found when the nation speaks and acts like God in His goodness and righteousness.

Arnold Toynbee in his comprehensive work, *The Study of History*, talked about the nineteen great civilizations that have collapsed. He makes an interesting point that only three of them were conquered by enemies from without. The other sixteen crumbled because of the weakness of the integrity of the people within the nation.

Edward Gibbon reached a similar conclusion in his classic, *The Decline and Fall of the Roman Empire*. Listen to the reasons that he listed for the downfall of mighty Rome: the rapid increase of divorce, belittling the sanctity of the home, higher and higher taxes while public money was wasted, a mad craze for pleasure, gigantic armaments for war, and the decline of religion into mere formality.

The security of a nation is experienced in the inner integrity of the people and not in the outer armaments of defense. Those who fought for the freedom of this nation wrote in our Declaration of Independence:

> We hold these truths to be self evident, that all men are created equal and that they are endowed by their Creator with certain inalienable rights. Appealing to the Supreme Judge of the world for the rectitude of our intentions, with firm reliance of the protection of Divine Providence, we mutually pledge to each other our lives, our fortunes, and our sacred honor.

How can one say it better than the framers of the Declaration of Independence? The security of our nation is found by living under the God who is good and righteous and who demands that His people express that goodness and righteousness to each other in their words and works. No one and no principality can conquer the righteousness of God. He proved that fact on the cross of Jesus Christ. The writer of Proverbs says, "The wicked are overthrown, but the house of the righteous shall stand."

The second reality which makes a nation secure is the counsel or purpose of the Lord. Listen to these verses of Psalm 33.

> The Lord brings the counsel of the nations to nought; he frustrates the plans of the peoples. The counsel of the Lord stands forever, the thoughts of his heart to all generations.

> Blessed is the nation whose God is the Lord, the people whom he has chosen as his heritage.

Here the psalmist speaks good news to a world which often feels, "These are the times that try our souls." The eyes of faith, according to the psalmist, perceive behind the disorder of national conflicts the invisible and invincible hand of God, who shapes the history of the world according to His eternal purpose. It is easy to see that the history of this world and the history of our nation are ultimately shaped by the purpose of God. Although great nations have dominated the world since antiquity and have devised clever effective plans, God has brought them to nought when they were at variance with His purpose. The people of Israel, whose own destiny was so tragically effected by the policies and actions of these kingdoms, and they learned from their own fate the one lesson that there is only one purpose which endures forever, and that is God's purpose.

We can find comfort for these trying times in the words of the psalmist, "The Lord brings the counsel of the nations to nought; he frustrates the plans of the peoples"

I agree with Robert Burns who says the best laid schemes o'mice and men can go astray when they are out of accord with the purpose of God.

What is the purpose of God? The psalmist tells us in verse twelve, "Blessed is the nation whose God is the Lord, the people whom he has chosen as his heritage." The purpose of God is election. The purpose of God is freedom. God calls humankind to be His people. In that call, we find freedom, freedom from the powers of sin and death.

According to the writer of I Timothy, God is our Savior, "who desires all men to be saved and come to the knowledge of truth." The truth that God desires all people to know is Jesus Christ, and He is the truth that makes us free. Another way to say this is to say that God's purpose is for all people to be free. Freedom comes when people know Jesus Christ the One who breaks the chains of sin and death and frees us to live the genuinely human life that God intended in the beginning of time.

The elect of the nation and the elect of the world have a clear responsibility. We are to tell the Good News that God desires all people to be saved. He has planned that they too should come and receive the freedom of Jesus Christ, freedom to be human like Christ in the fullest sense.

I discovered an astounding figure. Sixty million Christians now live in the Soviet Union. When we think about a possible nuclear war with the Soviet Union, we are talking about killing sixty million brothers and sisters in Christ, sixty million people whom God has elected as His own.

If the Christians of this nation and the Christians of the Soviet Union could somehow speak their Good News to each other and to our governments, the leaders of our nation and the leaders of the Soviet Union would have no choice but to beat our nuclear spears into plow shares. "The Word of God," according to the writer of Hebrews, "is quick and powerful, and sharper than any two-edged sword."

The security of our nation, then, is realized when we live within the purpose of God, when we live freely in Jesus Christ, and when we share God's purpose with the world. Security comes in sharing and telling the Good News of Christ. The good news is that God frustrates and brings to nought the plans of persons and nations who choose not to live within His purpose.

Finally, the third reality which makes a nation secure is the Providence of the Lord. Another way of saying this is to say, the nation is secure when it lives responsibly under the watchful eye of God.

Listen to these verses of the psalmist.

> The Lord looks down from heaven and sees all the sons of
> men; from where he sits enthroned he looks forth on all
> the inhabitants of the earth, he who fashions the hearts
> of them all, and observes all their deeds. A king is not
> saved by his great army; a warrior is not saved by his great

strength. The war horse is a vain hope for victory, and by its great might it cannot save. Behold, the eye of the Lord is on those who fear him, on those who hope in his steadfast love, that he may deliver their soul from death and keep them alive in famine.

These words of the psalmist remind us that whatever a nation does, it does it in the sight of the omniscient God and this reality accounts for the utter seriousness of our responsibility. The psalmist reminds us that we as a nation are watched by God, and that awareness should lead us to obedience.

The nation who is obedient to God can therefore believe that God is present and watching over His people. The security of a nation is found in the presence of God, in the watchful eye of the God of Israel, who neither slumbers nor sleeps.

A nation must put its trust in the all-powerful God, and not in powerful armies, powerful armaments and human strength. The psalmist says, "A king is not saved by its great army; a warrior is not saved by his great strength. The war horse is a vain hope for victory, and by its great might it cannot be saved."

Our nation's security does not exist in the great might of the war horse. As the psalmist says, "It is a vain hope for victory." One nuclear submarine carries enough warheads to destroy every major city in the Soviet Union. We can build one hundred of these submarines and one thousand MX missiles but such a storehouse of weapons cannot give our nation security because, according to the Word of God, "the war horse is a vain hope, and by its great might it cannot save."

Only God can grant deliverance and salvation. Only God can deliver a nation from death. The life of the nation is in God's hand and He can preserve us even in a calamity which cannot be overcome by humankind.

As a nation, we have put these words on our money, "In God we trust." Our nation was founded on that premise. Our freedom as a nation and our freedom as Christians were won on that premise. Our future can only be based on that premise.

The psalmist assures us that our security does not come in the might of the warrior. Rather it comes from our faith and trust in the omnipotent God, the all-powerful God, who reigns forever and ever, who destroys the wicked by the breath of His mouth.

The psalmist reminds us that the nation who trusts in God alone can be assured that the watchful eye of God is on them, and therefore they know that they are safe in His loving kindness. They are safe because God watches all nations. He thwarts and brings to nought the plans of those nations who do not live within His purpose.

Our security as a nation comes from the all-powerful God and not from the all powerful weapon. When we as a nation can trust in God alone, then we can look forward to the future without fear because we trust in One who cannot be defeated. From such faith flows strength which is greater than any strength we can find in the war horse. As Luther has written in one of his hymns, "A safe stronghold our God is still."

Yes, these are the times that try our souls, particularly when we discuss and debate the security of our nation. However, as we celebrate years of freedom in this great land, let us remember that our security is in God alone.

The psalmist concludes his festival hymn in this way.

> Our souls wait for the Lord;
>
> he is our help and shield.
>
> Yea, our heart is glad in him,
>
> because we trust in his holy name.

Prayer

Our fathers' God to Thee, Author of liberty, to Thee we sing, Long may our land be bright with freedom's holy light; Protect us by Thy might, Great God, our King, through Jesus Christ our Lord.

Peacefulness
Psalm 46
Mark 4:35-41

I stood at the fence which separated the lane from the lawn. When the cows came up for water, they often tried to nudge their noses through the square openings of the wire in order to taste the green grass of my grandparent's beautifully kept yard. That old fence had weathered many years of abuse from those curious cows who thought "the grass was greener on the other side," and thus that old dividing wall was not as sturdy as it once was.

I gingerly rested an elbow on one of the old rickety fence posts as I watched the storm clouds appear on the western horizon. I was fourteen at the time, and one of my favorite pastimes during those memorable months of summer on my grandparents' farm was to observe approaching storms which swiftly swept across the flat lands of Indiana.

Watching those mid-western storms always fascinated me. The lightning was similar to the laser show at Stone Mountain etching all kinds of different designs against the billowy, dark clouds, and the sound of the thunder seemed to hug the ground as it rolled across that level earth. Peacefully leaning against a fence post and looking at those approaching storms in the western skies always filled me with awe. Only the Creator could cause such beauty to transpire.

Suddenly I realized that this particular storm differed from others I had enjoyed. As it rapidly approached, the air became deathly still. The leaves on the trees hung limply from the limbs; the birds stopped their chirping and the roosters ceased their crowing. An eerie quietness prevailed.

Then I spotted it! A long, dark tail swooped and swirled across the distant field. Dust and debris dangerously danced in its path. I ran to the house to alert my grandparents and to seek shelter in an old dwelling which had endured many difficult days of storms in the past.

As the tornado approached with its deafening roar, we cowered in the corner of the cellar. I could hear the limbs snapping, and an old walnut tree next to the house fell to the ground with a loud thud! The timbers in that old dwelling creaked and cracked as the house swayed in the wind. My heart raced! I had never experienced such fear. As I tightly held my grandmother's hand, I could think of one prayer: "Lord, save us!" I must have uttered that prayer at least fifty times under my breath.

Strange, isn't it? How can something so mysterious and so beautiful suddenly become so destructive? As one reads the lesson from Mark's Gospel this morning, he wrestles with the same question: How can something so mysterious and as beautiful as the Sea of Galilee suddenly become so destructive?

Mark presents Jesus as the matchless teacher. He records four powerful parables of our Lord: The Parable of the Sower, the Parable of the Lamp under a Bowl, the Parable of the Growing Seed, and the Parable of the Mustard Seed. Immediately following the parables, Mark presents Jesus as the mighty Miracle Worker. He relates the four parables to the cycle of four of Jesus' miracles which are climacteric and complete. In our lesson for this morning, Mark shows Jesus' power over the forces of nature in the stilling of the storm. Next, he shows the Master's power over the demons of the spirit world in the healing of Legion. Then he reveals our Lord's power over the ravages of disease in the healing power over death in the raising of Jairus' daughter.

Mark sets the scene for us. The matchless teacher shares these four parables with the crowd, which is seated on a grassy knoll that hugged the shoreline of the Sea of Galilee. Our Lord used the bow of a boat for his pulpit. As we read the narrative, we see that the long day of teaching came to an end. As Mark says, "Evening had come." Needing a night of rest, Jesus instructed the disciples to sail to the other side of the lake.

Ostensibly, the sea was calm when they set sail. The boat probably belonged to Peter and Andrew or to James and John. The Galilean fishing boats were large and somewhat unwieldy, with one mast and one large, triangular sail. At the stern of the boat, just in front of the helmsman one found a small platform-like deck, and on it was a cushion where distinguished guests sat while the boat sailed.

During the peaceful evening journey, Jesus, according to Mark, sat on this cushion on the stern of the boat. Tired from the long day of teaching, our Lord soon fell asleep. Knowing full well the dangers of the Sea of Galilee and the fearful storms that suddenly and surprisingly strike from what seems out of nowhere, Jesus peacefully slept on the cushion in the stern because He trusted the skills and the resources of His fisherman friends.

Those of you have seen the Sea of Galilee can attest with me that it is probably one of the most beautiful spots on the face of the earth. One can only imagine the beauty of that moment. The large mountains loomed against the dark horizon. The stars in the vast vault above twinkled with glowing delight. The moon glistened on the soft ripples of the sea, while casting a golden glow on the nearby grain fields. Occasionally one could hear a school of fish popping the water, chasing frightened shad or feeding on low flying moths. It was a good night to sail, to think, and to sleep.

The surface of the Sea of Galilee is 680 feet below sea level. The lake and the surrounding area is like a deep basin in the earth, and because of its position, the lake is surrounded by deep gorges in the nearby mountains. As Barclay says, "If a cold wind comes from the west, it will rush down those narrow gorges and leap out onto the lake with startling suddenness, and the calm of one moment may well be the raging storm of the next."

As Mark tells us, the calm, glassy sea suddenly turned into a raging tempest. As the great wind swept down the deep gorges and churned the waters into dangerous angry waters, the boat soon began to take on the added weight of unwelcomed water from the washing of the waves. Yet Jesus continued to sleep comfortably on the cushion in the stern!

As our Lord slept peacefully, the disciples frightfully fought the great gale. At first the fearful men worked hard to save themselves and the vessel. Suddenly the storm that raged on the outside quickly worked its way to the inside, i.e., into their hearts. They were extremely afraid, and as they looked at their Master lying comfortably on a cushion asleep, they became indignant at his blissfulness in their moment of need. Finally, the disciples shook Jesus out of his sleep, and cried out, "Teacher, do you not care if we perish?"

One of the amazing facts about this incident is that most of these disciples were expert sailors who knew perfectly well how to handle a boat, especially in a violent storm on the lake. Yet, they appealed to Jesus who had never handled boats because he had worked with his father as a carpenter in Nazareth. How could an erstwhile carpenter aid these skilled sailors when all their experience meant nothing against the violent wind and death in the destructive waves was their certain fate? At the end of their resources, in which every sailor takes pride, the disciples threw themselves upon Jesus, the One who had never sailed a boat: "Teacher, do you not care if we perish?"

Anthony Bloom says that the disciples wanted Jesus to be anxious with them. Their words, "Do you not care if we perish?" really meant, "If you can do nothing, at least don't sleep. Die in anguish with us."

The absolute serenity of Jesus is astounding. That which caused a panic in the disciples did not cause a panic in Jesus. He calmly spoke one word to the raging wind and water. One can translate that Greek word, *pethimoso*, in this way: "Be still!"

Instantaneously the raging storm obeyed the one word command. Mark tells us that the wind immediately ceased, and "there came a great calm!" The rolling and rough sea, at the Master's command, became calm and serene again—as serene as the heart of Jesus.

The writer of Genesis tells us that in the beginning of time, the raging ocean which covered everything was engulfed in total darkness, and the breath of God moved over the waters. Suddenly God spoke one word and order came out of chaos.

Once again in Galilee the Creator of the universe spoke one word to the dark, churning sea, and order was restored to the chaotic waters of Galilee and to the chaotic hearts of the disciples. "There was a great calm!" In the words of the seventeenth century hymnist, "Fairest Lord Jesus, Ruler of All Nature."

Mark does not attempt to explain to his readers the common thought that storms were caused by demons. The word that Jesus spoke to the sea is the same word that he spoke to the demon in the beginning of the gospel. Martin Luther says it this way in his hymn,

"A Mighty Fortress is Our God."

> And though this world with devils filled, should threaten to undo us, we will not fear, for God has willed His truth to triumph through us. The prince of darkness grim, we tremble not for him; His rage we can endure, for lo! His doom is sure; One little word shall fell him.

What is that one little word? It is the word of Jesus, "Be still."

Most New Testament scholars warn preachers to avoid allegory in the case of this text. If we look at this passage in a strict literalistic fashion, then we do this marvelous account an injustice, and the words of Jesus, "Be still," remain quite external to us. However, if we read this passage with the eyes of symbolism, we see that this marvelous miracle of the stilling of the storm happens every day in our lives.

What person here this morning does not often experience a stormy life? Storms are within us almost daily! There are emotional storms, storms of illness, storms of impending death, storms of difficult decisions, storms of conflict, storms of painful separation, storms of temptation, storms of anxiety, and on and on! Lets face it: Life is often like the raging wind and sea that threatened the safety of the disciples.

When our storms continue in all of their fury, it sometimes appears that Jesus is sleeping indifferently while we suffer. So we spend our watchful hours communicating our despair to Him. It seems to me that we make the mistake of spending all of our time thinking about our fear and communicating our panic to the Lord of life rather than allowing Him to share His calmness with us.

Those of you who know me well can attest to the fact that I am not the most serene person in the world. I experience frustration, fear, anxiety, and worry as much as anyone else. Yet I learned an important lesson thirty-six years ago that I would like to share with you, if you will allow me to be personal.

In the summer of 1976, I suffered a mysterious illness which the doctors never diagnosed. For ten days, I experienced hard chills brought on by dangerously high fever. My physician prepared Judy for the worst, saying, "I do not know what he has, and I do not know what is going to happen to him."

In the few lucid moments that I experienced, I realized that I was in trouble. I was extremely afraid—and so was Judy!

One night before she went home from the hospital, Judy lay on the bed with me, resting her head on my shoulder. I am not sure whether it was her tears or mine which dropped on my feverish chest, perhaps both. In that moment as we held each other tightly and gazed out of the hospital window at the orange evening sky, we experienced a certain peace which we had never experienced in our married life and perhaps in our entire individual lives. As we held each other, we had the strange sensation of being held by someone else. The issue in that brief moment was not whether I was going to live or die. The issue was a peaceful calmness that would continue to hold us and to keep us no matter what the future brought.

I learned something very important from that experience;

God is always in the storm! God is always present with His peace! Perhaps His calmness can only come when our fretful mouths are closed in silence.

The psalmist says it this way:

> Therefore we will not fear though the earth changes, and though the mountains be shaken into the hearts of the seas, though the waters thereof roar and be troubled, through the mountains tremble with swelling thereof, The Lord of hosts is with us. The God of Jacob is our refuge.

Jesus said it this way: "Fear not I am with you always!"

One thing I am sure of, as sure as I am of the fact that today is Sunday; Jesus Christ is always in the midst of our storms, ready to calm our fearful anxieties with the peaceful command in His voice: "Be still." Such calmness is sheer grace. Peace is not something He owes us; rather it is something He gives to us because He loves us!

The matchless Teacher, the wonder-working Son of God is with us ready to speak, "Be still," ready to give calmness to our worry-filled lives, if we only stop fretting long enough to see and to hear His peace. "Be still," he said, "and suddenly there was a great calm."

Jesus spoke these words in one of His parables: "The rain descended, the floods came, and the winds blew and bear upon that house; and it fell not: for it was founded upon a rock" You and I are founded upon the rock, Jesus Christ. He is the Lord of nature and the Lord of life whose one word can still the force of any storm. Listen for it: "Be still."

When that one word comes, we shall be like the old farm house which creaked and swayed in the forceful winds of the tornado. Although weather-beaten, it remained standing in the calm aftermath, ready to provide safe dwelling for years to come.

Reformation and Righteousness
Romans 3:21-28

On a sultry summer day in A. D. 1505, Martin Luther, at the age of twenty-two, was returning to his studies at the University of Erfurt after a brief visit with his parents. Suddenly a severe thunderstorm unleashed its fury all around this vulnerable traveler. As a bolt of lightning struck dangerously close to him, the young Luther cried out, "St. Anne, help me! I will become a monk."

During the Middle Ages, most people were filled with fear and anxiety; they dreaded death and sought with all their might to find reconciliation with a God whom they feared. Philip Melanchthon, a disciple of Luther, once reported that the fear of God's wrath drove Luther into the monastery. Medieval people believed that monastic life, rightly lived, would guarantee one the right of eternal salvation.

Luther, along with most people who lived in the early days of the sixteenth century, had a warped view of God. Rather than experiencing God as the loving Savior in Jesus Christ, Luther viewed God as a stern and strict judge who demanded righteousness in men and women. The popular view in those days was that salvation was impossible unless believers performed good works that would please this stern, judgmental God. So Luther devoted himself to achieving righteousness; this young monk believed that he had to live a sinless, God-pleasing life in the monastery in order to find eternal bliss. In his book, *Four Reformers,* Kurt Aland quotes this famous passage from Luther's writings: "It is true that I was a pious monk and followed the rules of my order so faithfully that I may say if ever a monk could have entered heaven through monkery, it would have been I . . . and if I had had the time I would have martyred myself with vigils, prayers, readings, and other works."

Eugene Osterhaven, in his book, *The Spirit of the Reformed Tradition*, tells us that Luther sometimes confessed his sins six hours at a time, carefully racking his memory and searching his conscience in order to placate his stern and angry god; in hope that after such painful confession, eternal punishment might be averted. Writes Luther, "Though I lived as a monk without reproach, I felt that I was a sinner . . . I often repeated my confession . . . and yet my conscience could never give me certainty . . . I myself was more than once driven to the very abyss of despair so that I wished I had never been created. I hated this word, 'righteousness,' and I hated this just God who punished sinners (who could not attain righteousness)."

During his time as a monk, Luther earned his Doctor of Theology degree in 1512 and became a professor of Bible. As he prepared his lectures he wrestled with the first and third chapter of Romans. In Romans 1:17, the young professor read these words, "For in the gospel, the righteousness of God is revealed through faith." In Romans 3:28, Luther had to come to terms with our text for today: "For we hold that a man is justified by faith apart from the law." As Kenneth Latourette says in his book, *A History of Christianity*, "Light began to dawn by slow degrees as the prelude to dawn . . . until suddenly when the brilliant appearance of the sun broke upon Luther." The study of Romans brought the distraught monk the illumination by which he was to live. Luther discovered that we are saved by the grace of God in Jesus Christ and not by our attempts to earn the pleasure and favor of God. Luther's discovery helped him to see that through faith we sinners know Christ as Savior and are able to see the fatherly love of God. Luther still believed that God judged and condemned, but he realized that God yearned to save sinners and in Christ had provided a means by which salvation is accomplished. Wrote Luther, "And I extolled my sweetest word with a love as great as the hatred with which I had before I hated the words 'righteousness of God.' Thus that place in Paul was for me truly the gate to paradise."

Unintentionally and to his surprise, Luther's experience of justification by faith soon made him an important person in Germany and later in all of western Europe. Luther's preaching about the need for moral reform in the Church had an innocuous effect on the ecclesiastical hierarchy; however, he became the center of controversy when he challenged the sale of indulgences. Since the Crusades, people had been able to purchase an indulgence from the Church. It included the presentation of an Indulgence Letter, ornamented with the pope's signature, and the purchaser could have the assurance in black and white that his/her sins had been forgiven. In 1476 Pope Sixtus IV declared indulgences to be available and valid for the dead in purgatory as well as for the living. Fearful and anxious persons like the young Luther, before he discovered the truth of "justification by faith", could purchase an indulgence known as "plenary" and it was supposed to cover every possible sin, past or future. In 1516, Luther in his sermons questioned the efficacy of indulgences and emphasized that papal authority did not include the right to release souls from purgatory.

In 1517, indulgences were being hawked in Germany by a clever Dominican monk named John Tetzel. Tetzel boasted that he had saved more souls through the sale of indulgences than St. Peter had by preaching the gospel. In a "catchy" phrase, Tetzel proclaimed, "As soon as the coin in the coffer rings, the soul from purgatory springs." This peddler of indulgences announced that the proceeds were to aid in the new St. Peter's which the popes were building in Rome.

Tetzel's scheming tactics aroused Luther's ire, and on October 31, 1517, he posted on the door of the castle church in Wittenberg, which was like a university bulletin board, his ninety-five theses. In academic circles that was the normal procedure for obtaining a discussion or debate. The Reformation was born when Luther declared in his ninety-five theses that no good work or the purchase of indulgences has justifying merit. Rather salvation is a free gift of God made possible only through faith in the righteousness and atoning death of Jesus Christ. Luther's discovery of Paul's doctrine of "justification by faith" began a new era in the Church and in all of Christendom. Luther called this important doctrine "the article by which the church stands or falls," because he believed the interpretation of the gospel of Jesus Christ was at stake.

What did the doctrine of justification mean to Martin Luther and John Calvin? What meaning does it have for you and me today? What did the Apostle Paul mean when he wrote, "For we hold that a man is justified by faith apart from the law?" Rachel Henderlite writes these words in her book, *A Call to Faith*:

> The picture which the word (justification) calls to mind is that of a law court with all the dignity and solemnity of the law—the judge, the lawyers, the witnesses, the people, and the accused. The prisoner is brought to trial; the evidence is all against him. His is self-confessed guilt. But to the surprise of all present, the judge rises to his feet and announces in ringing, unmistakable words: "I declare this prisoner innocent of the charges leveled against him." And the prisoner is free in the face of crippling, damning evidence of his guilt. And no one can question his state, for the judge himself has pronounced him righteous.

In His amazing and incredible mercy and grace, God justifies us in Jesus Christ. Through Christ, God pardons us of our sin, accepts, loves, welcomes and treats us as if we had never been sinners at all. In Book III, Chapter XI of his *Institutes*, John Calvin said that "justification means nothing else than the acquit of guilt of him who was accused, as if his innocence were confirmed." I remember one of my pastors defining justification through a play on words. He said, "Justification is God's acceptance of us 'just-as-if' we had never sinned." The Apostle Paul said it this way in II Corinthians 5:19, "God was in Christ reconciling the world to himself, not counting their trespasses against them."

Justification is a state of pardon. Through Jesus Christ we are forgiven of our sins and restored to a new and right relationship with God. We experience justification through an act of God's grace in the Christ-event. One never has to earn the love, forgiveness, and acceptance of God, as the young Luther once thought. God's salvation is a free gift. In the New Testament lesson for this morning, we read these words of Paul, "Since all have sinned and fall short of the glory of God, they are justified by His grace as a gift, through the redemption which is in Christ Jesus."

God never says to us, "I will love you if you are good." Nor does He say to us, "I will love you if you do everything you are supposed to do." God's love is not conditional! Through the Reformation, we learned that we do not have to earn God's love because it is free. So God says to us, even this day, "I love you . . . I accept you . . . in spite of your unworthiness, in spite of your unlovableness." How can God love us with such an unconditional love? He is able to love and accept us because Christ has died for us, and He has restored us to a righteous or right relationship with God. To be justified is to be forgiven and accepted by God through the redeeming work of Jesus Christ, and this reality is the very essence of the Gospel.

In his book, *A History of Christian Thought*, Paul Tillich writes, "We are acceptable in the moment in which we accept acceptance."

The Apostle Paul says it this way in our text for today, "We are justified by faith." In other words, we experience acceptance when we accept God's love, when we accept Jesus Christ.

A friend of mine who is a minister in this area has been participating in a therapy group for ministers. Even ministers need help now and then. One minister in the group was in great emotional turmoil one day. Out of his inward struggle, he wept and said. "All I have ever wanted to do is to let God use me." The therapist, a kind and compassionate Christian, got up from his seat, went to the side of the sobbing minister and wrapped his arms around the shaking shoulders of the pastor. Gently he said, "God doesn't want to use you, He wants to love you."

Reformation Sunday and the doctrine of justification remind you and me that God wants to love us. The good news is that we do not have to prove ourselves worthy of God's love; we only have to reach out and accept it through Jesus Christ.

Prayer

Thanks be to You, our Father, for loving us in a way that we as humans are incapable of loving. We praise you for Jesus Christ who has made us acceptable in Your sight. Each day enable us to accept Your love through Him, Jesus Christ, our Lord. Amen

Saints and the Church

November 1 is All Saints Day, and the Sunday which follows All Saints Day is known as All Saints Sunday. The origin of our celebration goes back to the fifth century when the Barbarians were invading the Roman Empire.

As the church sought to convert these warring Barbarians, the Fathers of the faith had to deal with many of their pagan practices—one of which belonged to the Celts, who worshipped the sun.

On the last night of their calendar year—October 31—the Celtic priests dressed in white robes and sought to appease all the spirits of the dead.

The Celts believed that the souls of all those who had died during the previous year roamed the country side on the last night of the year, that is October 31, playing tricks on family members and friends whom they had left behind, hexing farm animals and stirring up storms.

Family members, according to the Celts, could calm these silent and suspicious spirits who roamed the country side by cooking their favorite foods and leaving it out on the front porch for them to discover. Thus one hoped to avoid a trick by offering the souls of the dead a treat and this is the origin of our children's trick-or-treat observance.

The Celts and Druids often mocked the insignias which they observed on the tombstones of Christians. One which the early Christians used was the skull and crossbones.

In fact, they mocked the Christians by gathering around a human skull and pretending to worship it. The Halloween pumpkin or Jack-o-lantern has its origin in the Celts' mocking reverence to the soul of one who had died represented by the burning candle inside the carved pumpkin.

During the fifth century, the church Fathers struggled to destroy the folklore of Halloween among the Barbarians, but they realized little success so the church simply incorporated this practice into its life and worship. They justified these observances by giving them a Christian meaning.

The Church continued this practice with other holidays as well: the Christmas tree, mistletoe, holly, and candles were all a part of the pagans' celebration of the winter solstice. The church was more interested in converting the Barbarians than it was in destroying all of their past so they took a pagan rite and Christianized it.

The early English name for All Saints Day was Hallows Day, All Holies Day. It was from this name that we receive the popular name for the preceding day Halloween or Evening of All Hallows.

The church, then, gave a Christian meaning to the ancient custom of the Celts, and enabled the new converts to see the importance of thanking God for the life of those on earth who have now entered the heavenly church, the Church Triumphant. And so we have All Saints Day and All Saints Sunday.

Last week we observed Reformation Sunday and Calvin followed Luther's practice of retaining the observance of All Saints Sunday, although both men rejected the saying of the mass for the dead.

The Reformers taught that prayers to God for the dead should be changed to prayers of thanksgiving for the life of the deceased, and beseech the God of compassion to comfort the family and friends left behind.

Once a person dies, he/she is in the hands of God, and thus all that one needs to say to the Lord of Heaven about the departed is what the church has said for over 2000 years: "Precious in the sight of the Lord is the death of his saints."

Before we go any farther, we need to ask the question, "Who or what is a saint?"

There are many definitions available:

"A saint is a dead sinner, revised and edited by the surviving relatives."

"A saint is a sinner who never got caught."

"A saint is a person of keen religious insight because of his experience as a sinner."

"A saint is a person who is particularly hard to get along with."

And yet when the Apostle Paul wrote his letter to the Corinthians, he addressed it "To all the Saints who are in Corinth."

And then when we read the chapters that follow, we see that Paul devoted most of the epistle lambasting the Corinthian saints for their vile behavior, immorality, lust, fornication, unfaithfulness to marriage vows, fighting, and getting drunk at the Lord's Supper.

And Paul dares to call these folks saints? What is a saint? Luther put it very simply: "A Saint is a redeemed sinner." Holy? Yes, absolutely holy. Righteous? Yes, absolutely righteous but not through his/her own works or their conduct. Our Lord has reminded us that no one is good but God. The Apostle Paul writes: "All of us have sinned and have come short of the Glory of God."

You are a sinner; I am a sinner; we are all sinners—but as Luther has said, "We are redeemed sinners—saints—people who trust solely in Jesus Christ for our salvation." A saint is a believer in Jesus, the Savior.

Now sainthood is not the act of the church nor the act of human. It is the act of God. We stand every Sunday in this hallowed place in the presence of the Holy God as worthless, dying, condemned sinners and simultaneously we stand holy, righteous, redeemed and reconciled before Almighty God.

We stand thus, not because of anything we have done but by the sheer grace and love and mercy of God through the suffering death, resurrection, and ascension of our Savior, Jesus Christ.

Thus when we refer to ourselves as the Communion of Saints or when we refer to ourselves individually as Saints, we are not saying, "Look how good we are." We are saying, "Look how good God is." Thus, the "Communion of Saints" means literally, "The Community of Believers".

On this All Saints Sunday, we celebrate one, great, unique mark of the Communion of Saints—one characteristic that makes the fellowship different than any other on earth—the quality that places it over and above all secular organizations that have ever existed or now exist.

This is the communion, this is the bond, this is the fellowship that bridges the gap between time and eternity. Death cannot destroy this communion, this fellowship with the saints of all ages.

On this All Saints Sunday, we attest to the faith and to the fact that our fellowship is a communion of eternal life. The members of this beloved community remain a part of it even after death.

Today, we have listed in our bulletins the names of three members who have entered into the Church Triumphant during the year of our Lord 1995. These precious persons as all the saints who have departed this church for the church above are still listed as members in the Session Minutes. There is no difference in the listing of members with exception of a notation that they now reside with the Risen

Lord of the Church.

You see, that is what makes belonging to the Church so exciting. The thrilling fact of the fellowship of the Church of Jesus Christ is as Paul reminds us that when we gather for worship, we are surrounded by a great cloud of witnesses, mother, father, brothers, sisters, spouses, children who have preceded us into the Church Triumphant are here with us now. And if we shut our eyes for a moment and listen we can see them and hear them.

When the church on earth stumbles and grovels its way along the sometimes torturous existence we remember that the Church rests on a living foundation of prophets, apostles, and martyrs, the eternal communion of saints who trust in the risen Lord Jesus Christ.

The church lost something very special in its life when it became an urban organization and established cemeteries. One of the things I enjoy about the Salem Black River Presbyterian Church is the beautiful cemetery behind the sanctuary.

The graves are a constant, visible reminder that those saints are still a part of the fellowship. Yet right here in this hallowed place we are reminded in the windows, on the pews, on the communion table, in the font, that the saints who went before us in this place are still a part of the family.

That is why this place can never be anything but a sanctuary, a place of the Sanctus, a place of that which is holy. There must always be an atmosphere of hallowed awesomeness about this edifice and everything that occurs in here must always maintain a sense of dignity because Jesus Christ is here with all his beloved children below and above. This is why we rededicate this sanctuary today a place of the holiness and saint. We all have tasted death and have experienced its pain.

The words of our Savior ring loud and clear: "Because I live you shall live also." The Apostle Paul reminds us that there is no difference between the faithful living and the faithful dead when he writes, "I would not have you be misunderstanding concerning those who are asleep, so that you don't sorrow as others, who have no hope."

So on this All Saints Sunday, we remind ourselves that we worship not only with the persons in this sanctuary this morning, not just in the fellowship of the millions who worship around the world today, but also with the millions upon millions who reside in the church above. We can see them we can hear them we can sense their presence because the Lord of life who has destroyed death's domain is here now.

One final thought needs to be shared concerning the meaning of this day. Somehow it reminds us that in the midst of life, you and I are moving steadily toward death but thank God we have been given the grace of Easter.

On a bright side, sunny April morning when lilies, azaleas, and dogwoods adorn this sanctuary, you and I are conditioned by our expectations of hearing the inevitable sermon on resurrection and life after death. We are also conditioned by the circumstances of the spring of the year, full of hope and buds and new blossoms—the spring of the year is a promise.

But in November? The sermons of dying and death—the days shortening, the darkness deepening, a long, cold winter ahead with dull skies, rain and perhaps ice? There is nothing in nature today to speak of new life and flowering hope. Yet on All Saints Sunday, we can sing out our Alleluias with more power and conviction than on Easter, because you and I are convinced beyond a shadow of a doubt that the Lord God omnipotent and the end of your life and mine is always guarded by God's triumphant, *Yes*.

One last word. Nicholas Beryaev writes a beautiful thought in his book *Destiny of Man*.

> Our attitude toward all people would be Christian, if we regarded them as though they were dying and [thus] determined our relationship with them in the light of their death. A person who is dying calls faith a special kind of feeling. Our attitude toward him/her is at once softened and lifted to a higher place. We then can feel compassion for people whom we did not love.

Imagine what this town and our nation and our world would be if each treated the other as a dying person. Truly it would be a life of compassion, and mercy, and peace.

Again, during another year, we have laid our saints to rest, these beloved persons who are still a part of this community. And so, in anticipation of our joining that great cloud of witnesses, at a time that only the Lord knows, we honor them, and we rejoice. We honor the

Christ who has raised them to life eternal. We re-dedicate this place and ourselves to the risen Lord Jesus.

Prayer

We thank You, O Lord that we belong to you and to one another. Perfect our lives and our communion with one another that we may one day join that great multitude in heaven which no one can number, standing before the throne of the Lamb, proclaiming, "Salvation belongs to our God." Amen.

The Inexpressible Gift
Isaiah 55: 6-11
II Corinthians 9: 1-15

In Indian folklore, one finds a tale about a small tribe of Indians who lived in Mississippi many years ago. They had built their teepees on the bank of a large river, and the river's current was so swift and deadly that even the strongest men in the village refused to cross it for fear of being swept downstream and drowned.

One day another tribe of hostile Indians attacked the peaceful village. The invaders greatly outnumbered the small tribe and soon backed them up to the river. The defeated villagers had no place to flee except into the swift waters; their only hope of survival was to attempt a crossing of the treacherous river. The stronger braves put the weaker members of the tribe on their shoulders and waded into the river. Amazingly the weight of another person on their shoulders kept the stronger braves from losing their footing, and everyone was able to cross the perilous channel without harm.

The point of this tale is fairly clear: The community survives difficult moments when the stronger members are willing to carry not only their own weight, but also the weight of someone else who is not as strong. In our New Testament Lesson for today, we find the Apostle Paul making that same point: he urges the saints, i.e., the believers in Corinth, to give an offering, as the churches of Galatia and Macedonia were doing, for the purpose of alleviating the poverty of some of the saints in Jerusalem. The stronger members of the Christian community could ease the suffering of the weaker ones by carrying those who suffered on their shoulders until times improved. I am not a fan of rock music, but I remember a certain phrase of a song that was recorded about six years ago, and I think Paul would have liked it: "He ain't heavy; he's my brother."

To fully grasp the meaning of today's text, one needs to know something about Paul's visits to Corinth and also something about his correspondence to the church there. In the eighteenth chapter of Acts, Luke informs us that Paul, on his second missionary journey left Athens and came to Corinth where he stayed with two tentmakers, Aquila and his wife Priscilla. In his book, *Toward the Understanding of St. Paul*, Donald Selby says that Paul probably began to organize this collection for the saints in Jerusalem during this eighteen month stay in Corinth.

After leaving Corinth, Paul began his third and final missionary journey. In C.A.D. 52-54, he traveled to Ephesus where he wrote his first letter to the Corinthians. Unfortunately that letter is no longer extant; it has been lost. However, in the letter that we now have as First Corinthians, which is really the second letter that Paul wrote to Corinth, he mentions his first letter in 5:9, "I wrote to you in my letter not to associate with immoral men." After the Corinthians had received Paul's first letter, they wrote him back and reported the deteriorating conditions of the church. In response to the difficult problems that the Corinthians were experiencing, Paul wrote a second letter which we now have as First Corinthians.

Later the concerned apostle sent Timothy to Corinth in an attempt to help the struggling Corinthians settle some of their problems. Months later Timothy returned to Paul at Ephesus, reporting that his efforts had failed and that the conditions in Corinth had grown worse. So Paul made a brief but painful visit to Corinth, hoping that his admonishment would correct the errant ways. However, the apostle did not receive a warm welcome: he suffered some serious abuse from one person in the church, and the remainder of the congregation acted defiantly. Some of Paul's opponents had come to Corinth in order to discredit him and to turn the people's allegiance away from the apostle. Humiliated and angry, Paul returned to Ephesus and wrote a third letter to Corinth known as the "severe letter." Paul tells us about this "severe letter" in II Corinthians 2:4: "For I wrote you out of much affliction and anguish of heart and with many tears."

Anxiously Paul waited for the return of Titus who delivered the "severe letter" to Corinth. Unable to wait patiently, Paul traveled to Macedonia where he met Titus, the "bearer of good news." After reading the "severe letter," the Corinthians mourned their errant ways, repented of their evil doings, and longed to see Paul. Upon hearing this good news, Paul wrote a fourth letter to Corinth which we have today as II Corinthians. The first nine chapters appear to be the essence of this fourth letter which one can appropriately call the "joyful letter." Our lesson today is a part of this fourth letter.

During the long and difficult months in which Paul and the Corinthians were at odds after his painful visit, that congregation had neglected the apostle's attempt to raise an offering for the poor of Jerusalem. Now that reconciliation had occurred, Paul hoped that the Corinthians would join the Macedonians and Galatians in this offering. In his book, *Interpreting the New Testament,* James Price tells us that Paul's motives for collecting this offering ran deeper than a humanitarian sympathy for the plight of the poor saints in Jerusalem. In Romans 15: 26-27, Paul explains the meaning of this endeavor:

> For Macedonia and Achaia have been pleased to make some contribution for the poor ... they are indebted to them, for if the Gentiles have come to share in the spiritual blessings of those in Jerusalem, then the Gentiles ought to be of service to them in material blessings.

Paul saw the collection for Jerusalem as a symbol of the church's unity. Through this concrete expression of love, the Jerusalem Christians, who often would discredit the faith of gentiles, would be made aware that the gentile Christians belonged with them as members of the Body of Christ. As Paul wrote, "If one member suffers, all suffer together." (I Corinthians 12:26)

Look with me now at the fifteen verses in chapter nine as Paul talks about what a difference the liberal giving of the Corinthians will make in their own lives and particularly in the lives of the church members in Jerusalem. Paul begins chapter nine by saying, "Now it is superfluous for me to write to you about the offering for the saints." In other words the apostle did not need to make the Corinthians aware of this great need in Jerusalem. They had known about it since the time of Paul's first visit to them. What the Corinthians needed was encouragement to speed up the collection. It had lagged during the time that Paul and the congregation were at odds with each other.

In verse two Paul continued, "For I know your readiness, of which I boast about you to the people of Macedonia, saying that Achaia (i.e the Roman province of Greece) has been ready since last year; and your zeal has stirred up most of them." One may ask, if the rift between Paul and the Corinthians had just been healed, how could the apostle boast about Corinth's readiness to give? The readiness to which the apostle refers is the initial response of the Corinthians when Paul first introduced the need to them.

Ostensibly their response was so overwhelming that Paul was touched, and he shared the generosity of Corinth with the churches of Macedonia. I find it interesting that Paul had intended to exclude the Macedonians from contributing to this offering because they too were plagued by poverty. However when they heard about Corinth's zeal for giving, the Macedonians insisted on making a contribution.

Individuals and individual churches do make a difference when they see themselves as leaders who are called to set examples. The Corinthian example can be our example in coming years. When people see our faith, our readiness to help, our generosity, they may be inspired to join in the service of Jesus. In other words, I expect our congregation to set examples for the presbytery and for this community.

One notices that verses three and four reveal an uneasiness in Paul. Although he had boasted about the readiness of Corinth, he vividly remembered the painful rift and feared that the Corinthians may not be as ready as they were when Paul first introduced to them the idea of an offering. So Paul tactfully wrote, "But I am sending the brethren so that our boasting about you may not prove vain in this case, so that you may be as ready as I said you would be; lest if some Macedonians come with me and find that you are not ready, we be humiliated—to say nothing of you—for being so confident."

In other words, Paul was saying, "I am concerned for my own good name and for yours. I made a promise in your behalf, and we will both be disgraced if your deeds and my words do not agree." A congregation's Christian name is always at stake when they are called upon to be generous—as generous as the Christ whom they serve.

In verse five, Paul wrote, "So I thought it necessary to urge the brethren to go on to you before me and arrange in advance for this gift you have promised, so that it may be ready not as an exaction but as a willing gift." In the previous chapter (8:16), Paul tells us that one of the brethren is Titus, but he does not identify the other two by name. Paul's purpose of sending Titus and the brethren to Corinth was not only to deliver this fourth letter, but also to begin making arrangements for the collection of the offering for the poor.

Paul wanted the Corinthians to be generous in their giving to the offering for Jerusalem. He did not want their giving to be done on the spur of the moment in response to a strong, emotional appeal that he would have to make if the collection were not ready when Paul came to Corinth. If that were the case, the apostle was afraid that people might feel as if Paul were pressuring them to give. He wanted the Corinthians to give out of their own desire to help someone in need because God had also helped the people of Corinth throughout the past years.

The brethren whom Paul sent were to help the Corinthians to understand that their gift must not be spontaneous, but rather it must be thoughtfully considered in light of what God had done for the Corinthians, in light of the impoverishment of some of the Christians in Jerusalem, and in light of their own financial situation and ability to give. Paul seems to imply that one's giving must always be intelligent and deliberate. That which usually makes people stingy is not a lack of desire to give and help, it is usually due to lack of thought.

In his book, *Matters of Life and Death*, Louis Valbract tells the story of how Judge Russell Lowell had been served oatmeal for breakfast every morning for twenty-six years because oatmeal was the proper breakfast for proper Bostonians. One morning tragedy struck; the judge's wife burned the oatmeal. Embarrassed, she said, "Russell, I burned the oatmeal and there is not a speck more in the house. For the first time in twenty-six years, I won't be able to serve you oatmeal for breakfast. Judge Lowell glanced up from his paper and said, "Quite all right. Never liked the stuff anyway." It had never occurred to the judge to think about his breakfast for twenty-six years.

Thoughtfulness must precede giving! Do you and I make our pledges for 1981 because we have been doing so out of habit for twenty-six years and even longer? Or do we truly think about the reason we give and the difference our gifts can make: "Is my gift generous? Does it reflect God's generosity to me? Does it reflect my gratitude for God's goodness? Is it large enough to make a difference in helping others? Is it proportionate to my ability to give? Have I given all that I can or have I held back?" Those appear to be some of the questions the brethren might have asked the Corinthians.

In verse six, Paul wrote: "The point is this: he who sows sparingly will also reap sparingly, and he who sows bountifully will also reap bountifully." Ostensibly some of the Corinthians feared that generous giving might cause them to suffer want later. Most people who are challenged to give have those fears. Yet Paul points out the reality of the farmer: if he limits the amount of seeds he plants, he limits the bounty of the harvest. Jesus once said, "The measure you give will be the measure you receive." One of the proverbs confronts us with a timely reminder: "Cast your bread upon the waters and it will return to you." Our Lord urged the kind of giving that expects nothing in return, but the law of returns remains: we reap what we sow! Paul was convinced that God would prosper the generosity of the Corinthians so that they might continue to help others in need. One has never become poorer for giving to God.

In verse seven Paul writes, "Each one must do as he has made up his mind, not reluctantly or under compulsion, for God loves a cheerful giver." Once again Paul emphasized that each Corinthian should give because he/she wants to give and not because the apostle wants them to, or because they feel Paul is putting pressure on them, or because they fear Paul will embarrass them if they do not give generously.

In Decatur Presbyterian Church, our stewardship theme has been "Witness 156." In celebration of 156 years of ministry for Jesus Christ in Decatur, the stewardship committee has invited the members of the congregation to consider giving at least $156 more than last year. Due to fixed incomes, some will not be able to consider that request. Others, whose income continue to escalate, can give a one-time gift of 10 or 20 times $156 over and above last year's pledge. Yet each of us must do as we have made up our mind, not reluctantly because the church has requested it, but because we want to do something for God and His Christ.

Paul reminded the Corinthians that "God loves a cheerful giver." The Greek word for "cheerful" is *hilaros*, from which we get our English word, "hilarious." God loves a hilarious giver, a light-hearted giver, who neither figures nor calculates how much the gift will set him/her back, but who gives generously out of love for God.

In interest of time, I am going to say very little about verses 8-12 because they are similar in thought to verse 6. Paul wanted to emphasize once again that God rewards generous giving with spiritual and material prosperity in order that the giver may continue to help God's children in need who will offer up thanksgiving to God because of the generosity of the giver.

Now look, if you will, at verse 13: "Under the test of this service you will glorify God by your obedience in acknowledging the gospel of Christ, and by the generosity of your contribution for them and for all others." In his commentary, John Calvin says that Paul reminds the Corinthians that their gift for the poor saints at Jerusalem is really a test of faith, that rightly passed, will give proof that the Corinthians sincerely believe and follow the gospel.

In one of his books, Charlie Shedd tells a story about a minister who was baptizing one of his new converts in a creek. As the neophyte approached the minister, he suddenly remembered something. "Just a minute," he said as he hastily ran back out of the water, "I forgot to give my wallet to my wife."

"Come back here," shouted the minister in a voice for all to hear, "I've already got too many unbaptized pocketbooks in our congregation."

The generous wallet or checkbook is the truest confession of faith I know. There are many people in Christendom today who are basic in their theology, who accept the doctrines of the church, who are faithful in observing rules about Christian living, who have a zeal for evangelizing, who know the Bible from cover to cover, who profess to love Jesus Christ with all their heart, and yet, "pinch their pennies" when it comes to giving to God. Maybe our wallets do need baptizing! According to Paul, our giving to God is really a test of faith, that rightly passed, will give proof that we believe and follow the gospel.

In verse 15, the apostle brings to a conclusion his thoughts on giving to the collection for the saints at Jerusalem. He vividly expresses the reason why the Corinthians should give an offering for Jerusalem: "Thanks be to God for his inexpressible gift." The rationale for Christian giving is the inexpressible gift of God to us in Jesus Christ. in the preceding chapter Paul said it this way: "For you know the grace of our Lord Jesus Christ, that though he was rich, yet for your sake He became poor, so that by His poverty you might become rich."

I have always admired the fifteenth century painting, entitled, "The Resurrection," by the Italian painter Francesca. The scene in the painting is Easter morning, just at dawn, as Christ is rising from the tomb. At the base of the sepulcher sleep four Roman soldiers, resting on their spears and shields. Caesar's men, who have been sent to guard the tomb, are asleep, blind to the miracle that is taking place in their midst. Their assumption that Caesar had the last word about Jesus is wrong.

Above the sleeping soldiers, Christ rises from death. The wounds of the crucifixion are still visible in His side, hands, and feet, The foot of the risen Christ is placed firmly on the tomb and over his shoulder He carries the flag of the Church Triumphant. However it is the shoulders of the risen Christ, which Francesca has painted, that have always captured my attention. They appear to be muscular and strong after hanging from the cross.

As the Indians in Mississippi carried the weaker member of the tribe on their shoulders through the dangerous and swift waters of the river, so our Christ has carried us on His shoulders through the swift waters of sin and death. Through Christ we have been made immune to sin and spiritual death. He is the inexpressible gift of God; He is the sole reason for any monetary gift. May our 1981 stewardship response reflect the gratitude of St. Paul and our gratitude for God's inexpressible gift in Jesus Christ.

Prayer

For the grace of liberality, for the opportunity to help others,
for the chance to prove our faith through giving, we give You
thanks, our Father. Increase, O Lord, our gratitude for the
inexpressible gift of Jesus Christ, and increase our zeal and
our ability to give of ourselves and of our resources for the sake of
Jesus Christ and His Kingdom. Amen.

The Final Chapter Is Not Final
Psalm 46: 1-7
Luke 11: 29-33

Recently I have been about the task of writing my autobiography. Fear not: I am not delusional. This autobiography is not for publication. Rather, I write so my grandchildren and great-grandchildren may know something of their ancestor and his life's ups and downs. These writings are contained in a special notebook. They are all written in long-hand. No need to mess up something with a computer.

Today's sermon is based on Chapter Three of that autobiography. Let me begin by saying: each of us has a Chapter Three in his or her life where pain poisons peace and prosperity.

So, Chapter Three begins in this manner. The passage of forty-three years often diminishes and dulls one's memory. Time, like an ever flowing stream, bears all our thoughts away. However, there are some things I remember keenly about that hot, muggy August day back in 1962.

Our Junior High Fellowship went on an outing to Sesquicentennial State Park on the Twenty Fifth of August. In those days, churches rarely had a van or a bus so mothers would volunteer to help transport youth and children to special events. My mother drove our family car that day. I rode with a friend's mother, but my brother, Earl, age nine, and my brother John David, age four, rode in our family car with my mother.

We had a delightful day of swimming and playing softball, not to mention the wonderful food prepared by the mothers of the youth. When it was time to depart, I announced to my mother and friends that I was driving home. In those days, one could get a driver's permit at fourteen.

My mother poured cold water on my pronouncement by saying something like, "You'll drive home over my dead body." Mothers have a way of messing up our plans.

I responded to her chilling remarks by saying, "You are the meanest mother in the world, and I hate you." Little did I know that these words would be the last words that I ever spoke to my mother.

The apostle said, "Be angry, but do not sin. Don't let the sun go down on your anger." How I wish I knew the meaning of Paul's words in those days, and I wish I could take those hateful, teenage words back and bury them in the sands of time.

Angry with my mother for refusing to allow me to show off my driving skills to my adolescent buddies, I rode home with my best friend and his mother. The trip home was uneventful for our car, but it was life-changing for my father, Earl, and for me. I stood in the churchyard all alone waiting for my mother to pick me up. Fifteen minutes passed, thirty, forty-five, one hour. As each car came around the curve on Monticello Road, I was sure it was she—only to be disappointed by the sight and sound of a stranger's car approaching, then passing, leaving me alone to my thoughts concerning the whereabouts of my mother and brothers.

Even at fourteen I had very little patience. Patient waiting has never been one of my virtues. The hot summer sun beat down on my head, burning the bald spot in my flattop haircut, while perspiration beaded up on the butch wax. The humidity was so high that my bleeding madras shirt bled on my chest that now was puffed up in anger.

Now my anger intensified as I waited without explanation and once again it was expressed in inappropriate words under my breath—inappropriate language that fourteen year old boys speak slyly but proudly as though its usage makes them men. At least I uttered them under my breath. After all, I was standing in the churchyard only 100 feet from the sanctuary.

Finally, I sought refuge from the summer sun under one of the majestic oak trees which grew along Monticello Road. Forgetting my starched Khaki pants and finely polished fake Weejuns, I sat on the ground where the shade had prevented the grass from growing and I doodled with my finger in the cool dirt. Jesus doodled in the dirt and said something about "He who was without sin".

One hour and fifteen minutes . . . one hour and a half. "Where in the world could that woman be?" I asked myself and God. How could she make me wait so unmercifully? Unless, she was trying to teach me a lesson for talking so ugly to her right before we left to go home.

Finally, a familiar car pulled into the churchyard revealing the friendly face of a neighbor. However, my heart pounded and my stomach churned when I saw clearly her distraught countenance. She and my mother had been childhood friends and now she had the unsavory task of telling me that my mother and brother were dead. They had been killed instantly in an automobile/train accident.

The shock of such startling and sad news left me incredulous. "NO! NO! NO! You're wrong. You're mistaken. My mother is not dead, she's just late."

No tears, no crying, just more inappropriate behavior demanding that this neighbor take me to my mother. In her own brokenness, she did.

The accident occurred at the RR crossing on Farrow Road in Columbia and when we finally arrived there, a crowd of people still lingered at the sight, mostly black folk who were scared and shocked by such a gruesome sight of mangled metal and human flesh.

I jumped out of the car even before it came to a full stop, running as quickly as I could to the frightening scene. Never have I been so swift of foot, but adrenalin does strange things to you in moments like those sickening moments forty-three years ago. As I raced toward the crossing, I tripped and fell at the feet of this kind, heavy-set lady who was dressed in white shoes and a white uniform.

She reached down to help me up. "Child, you better be careful," she said.

Looking desperately into her concerned eyes, I shouted, "Please, tell me, was anyone hurt in that accident?"

"Yes, child," she replied, "A mother and her baby were killed. Tragic, tragic, tragic, child. Just tragic."

Silently, I collapsed into her grasp, holding her huge flabby arms and whispering through my tears, "That was my mother and younger brother."

This kind lady held me to her breast as if I were her own son. Different colors of skin meant nothing to her or me. She just held me, wiped my forehead, and then she whispered, "Child, the Lord will take care of you and He will get you through, I know He will."

Each of us has a Chapter Three in his or her life where pain poisons peace and prosperity.

Let us look at a Chapter Three in this manner: Frederick Beuchner is his book, *The Clown in the Belfry*, tells this life occurrence.

> *After a good deal of drinking, my father decided to take the car and go driving off with it somewhere. My mother told him that he was in no condition to drive, and she would not give him the keys. I had already gone to bed, and she came*

upstairs to give the keys to me. She told me that under no circumstance was I to let my father have them.

Somehow or other my father found out that I had the keys—I can only assume that she told him—and he came upstairs to ask me for the keys. He sat down on one of the twin beds, and I was lying on the one next to it with the covers over my head—and the keys in my hand under the pillow.

For what seemed an endless time, he sat there pleading with me to let him have them, and I lay there under the covers, not saying anything because I no more knew what to say than I know what to do or be. I think I finally just went to sleep with the sound of my father's pleading in my ears and the keys, which I never gave him, still clinched tightly in my fist under the pillow. The child that I was certainly felt the pain of it, as attested to by the fact that I have so long remembered it.

One day a couple of summers ago, I read those few pages out loud to a group of some 60 people at a religious retreat in Western Texas. I could see that they were moved by my experience as I read it not because I had written it with any particular eloquence but because, as best as I could, I had written it in simple language of a child in a way that must have awakened in them similar painful memories of their own childhood.

When I finished reading, a man named Howard Butts came up and said a few words to me that opened my eye to see something that I had never clearly seen before. He said, "You have a good deal of pain in your life and you have been a good steward of it."

For me that is an astounding thought: "You have been a good steward of life's pain." I am not sure that I understand what those words mean. I do not know if I understand how one manages life's pain, but I know that all of us have difficult chapters in our lives.

For me, another chapter began five years ago when I was diagnosed with Parkinson's Disease—Chapter Ten. I'm still learning what it means to live with such an aggravating illness.

So I read what others, particularly people of great faith, do to overcome life's pain. George Hunsinger writes these words in *Theology Today*:

> "Beset by a dizzying array of illnesses, John Calvin lived in constant pain. The list of what he suffered included chronic gout, kidney stones, pulmonary tuberculosis, painful breathing caused by pleurisy, the coughing up of blood, recurring fevers, intestinal parasites, and migraine headaches. He died of Toxic Shock at age fifty-five."

How does one endure, how does one fulfill life's calling when plagued by such pain? How did Calvin manage his illnesses? How was he a good "steward of pain?" Besides his illnesses, Calvin knew grief and the loss of those whom he loved. His son died in infancy, the only child born to him and his beloved wife Idelette. Her death soon followed.

"I do what I can," wrote Calvin "that I might not be altogether consumed with grief. I have been bereaved of the best companion of my life. She was the faithful helper of my ministry." Only forty years old when she died, Calvin had to face fifteen years without her.

George Husinger continues, "Chastened by bitter experience and instructed by God's word, Calvin never over promised what the faithful should expect in life." The Gospel's promise was not necessarily one of health and prosperity. It was the promise of sustenance in the midst of afflictions.

Calvin wrote these words in *Book Three of the Institutes*:

> Various diseases repeatedly trouble us: now plaque rages; now we are cruelly beset by the calamities of war; now ice and hail, consuming the year's expectation, lead to barrenness, which reduces us to poverty; wife, parents, children, neighbors, are snatched away by death; our house is burned by fire.

Chapter Ten. But in these matters, the believer must also look to God's kindness and truly fatherly indulgence. Calvin continues:

> That God has promised to be with believers in tribulation they experience to be true, while, supported by His hand, they patiently endure, an endurance quite unattainable by their own effort.

In his commentary on Acts 13, Calvin writes,

> And there is no doubt that if our faith is properly founded on God and strikes its root deeply in His Word, and finally, if it is made thoroughly secure by the protection of the

Spirit, as it ought to be, it will foster peace and spiritual joy in our minds, even when the whole world is in an uproar.

Chapter Ten.

If I understand Calvin, it seems to me that he managed his pain through the grace of God which is received through the power of God's Word and Holy Supper. History speaks to this Reformer saying, "John Calvin, you have had a great deal of pain in your life and you have been a good steward of it."

One might say those same words to the Apostle Paul who wrote to the Corinthians.

> Three times I have been beaten with rods. Five times I have received the 40 Stripes less one. Once I was stoned. Three times I have been ship wrecked. A night and a day I have been shipwrecked. In my journeys I have been in perils of rivers, in perils from robbers and thieves, in perils in the wilderness, in perils of the sea.
>
> Then I suffered from the thorn in the flesh (epilepsy, severe headaches, poor eye sight, high fever).
>
> Three times I appealed to the Lord to remove these thorns from me but the Lord said my grace is sufficient for you. My power is made perfect in weakness.

Grace is the power which Christ gives to us when we experience human pain and struggles so that we can courageously face and endure life's problems. Grace is Christ's power to help us. So, by God's grace, the final chapter is not final.

Prayer

The grace of our Lord Jesus Christ, the love of God, and the communion of the Holy Spirit be with you now and forevermore.

Amen

Made in the USA
Lexington, KY
27 September 2015